LOCOMOTION PAPERS

Carrying Coals to Dunston

Coal and the Railway

by

Ernest Manns

THE OAKWOOD PRESS

© Oakwood Press & Ernest Manns 2000

British Library Cataloguing in Publication Data
A Record for this book is available from the British Library
ISBN 0 85361 560 8

Typeset by Oakwood Graphics.
Repro by Ford Graphics, Ringwood, Hants.
Printed by Cambrian Printers, Aberystwyth, Cerdegion.

Dedication

**For my father Ernest Manns, Pump Attendant, Dunston Power Station
and my father-in-law Thomas Halliday, Trimmer, Dunston Staiths**

Title page: A 'Q6' class 0-8-0 (ex-NER class 'T2') turning onto the Gateshead Link line with coal empties from Dunston Power Station in 1966. The Dunston Extension line from Low Fell is in the foreground and the Norwood signal box in the distance. Upper quadrant semaphores and colour light signals have replaced the original NER types.

A.R. Thompson

Published by The Oakwood Press (Usk), P.O. Box 13, Usk, Mon., NP15 1YS.
E-mail: oakwood-press@dial.pipex.com
Website: www.oakwood-press.dial.pipex.com

Contents

Foreword

Carrying coals to Newcastle has long been proverbially regarded as a pointless exercise, but nevertheless virtually all the coal which came from Newcastle and Tyneside had to be carried to the River Tyne itself before it could be exported. The waggonways and railways which carried the coal to the shipping ports on the river were an essential link in the transport of coal from the collieries to London, the main market for Tyne coal. The village of Dunston-on-Tyne, until recently a major port on the river, has a continuous record of railway activity, largely for the transport of coal, for over three and a half centuries. The history of the railways of Dunston and the Whickham/Pontop/Tanfield region of North-West County Durham illustrates the way in which the railway fostered and maintained the growth of industry and trade throughout Victorian times and until the mid-20th century when coal and steam were the primary source of energy. The coal trade, in developing the railway to overcome its local transport problems, produced a transport system which was itself to become a major industry and change the social, commercial and industrial life of the world.*

The Redheugh branch passes below the lines leading to Dunston staiths in 1969. Dunston East signal box, a bridge cabin, straddles the lines, and controls the siding access into the premises of the Co-operative Wholesale Society. The footbridge is now preserved at the North of England Open Air Museum at Beamish. Dunston East Jn was a location where the author spent many happy hours observing the railway as a boy.   *John Mallon*

* See *The World the Railways Made* by Nicholas Faith, Pimlico, 1990.

Acknowledgements

Ideally, historical writing should be based on research using primary sources. This book has been written in New Zealand, some twelve thousand miles from its subject region, and I have necessarily been greatly dependent upon previously published material supplemented by my own observations, notes and memories of the period between the late 1930s and 1960s. Whatever interpretations and conclusions I have based upon this material and any factual errors are of course my own. A key to the maps that illustrate this book is shown below.

Publications that have been of particular value are *A Fighting Trade* by Bennett, Clavering and Rounding for the history of the early waggonways and the people who built them; *Early Wooden Railways* by Lewis for technical details of the waggonways and their operation; and Tomlinson's *North Eastern Railway* and the many publications of the late Ken Hoole and of the North Eastern Railway Association for the later history of rail in the region.

I am greatly indebted to Henry Wilson, Bookseller of Chester, for the wide range of books, both current and out of print, which he has supplied with speed and friendly efficiency. The staff of Ashburton District Library (NZ), particularly Adrienne Moodie, tracked down a number of useful items which I did not expect to find in New Zealand. I am grateful to my sister Pat who obtained for me copies of various maps from the Gateshead Borough Library and to the library staff who gave her every assistance. I am grateful to those members of the North Eastern Railway Association who read and commented on the typescript, especially to Stan Wolfe whose advice and encouragement have been invaluable, and to Mike Ellison for his many constructive comments and suggestions. I am greatly indebted to Jim Lawson and Nicola Mills of the North of England Open Air Museum at Beamish and Alan Thompson of the Tanfield Railway (J.W. Armstrong Trust) for selecting and supplying photographs from their respective collections, and also to John Mallon for his photographs and for providing the information which is found in *Appendix Two*.

Map Symbols

Collieries	●
Farms	■
Industrial area	/////
Known wainways	— — —
Residential area	▦
Roads	– – – – –
Staiths	◢
Waggonways, railways	▬▬▬

Dunston Colliery officials - Messrs Walmsley, Surtees, Luke and Lawson; some of the men who made it all possible, 'the lads of coaly Tyne'.

Beamish Museum

Chapter One

Coal and the Railway

Throughout the period from the accession of Queen Victoria in 1837 until the middle of the 20th century, railways and coal together were the foundation on which the industrial and commercial prosperity of Britain was built.

The industrial revolution of the 18th century was based on water power. Water wheels drove the textile mills of Yorkshire and Lancashire and the forges and workshops of the Midlands, while throughout much of the country a network of canals provided the means of heavy transport beyond the capacity of the horse and the inadequate roads of the time. The subsequent development and expansion of industry and commerce throughout Victoria's long reign were based upon coal and the railway.

Between 1831 and 1901 the population of Britain (excluding Ireland) more than doubled, increasing from 16 million to 37 million; that of London, by far the largest city, had reached over 4½ million by 1901. They travelled by steam train, coal heated their houses, hospitals and hotels, brewed their beer, baked their bread and fired their bricks and pottery. Coal was converted to gas and coke and a host of by-products by the expanding chemical industry. Victorian engineering demanded vast amounts of iron - coke smelted the ore and coal fired the forges and foundries. The coal-fired stationary steam engine pumped water and sewage, powered the steel mills and machine shops and increasing numbers of the previously water-driven spinning mills and weaving sheds. By the early years of the 20th century coal-burning power stations* equipped with Sir Charles Parson's steam turbines, were generating the electricity to power city tramway systems, the London Underground, and suburban railways in the South East and on Tyneside. Industry was turning to the convenience and flexibility of the electric motor. The electric light bulb, invented independently by Sir Joseph Swan and the American Thomas Edison, was steadily replacing the older gas lamp. The greater part of the British merchant fleet, by far the largest in the world, steamed the oceans on coal and, as likely as not, refilled their bunkers on exported British coal stocked at one of a worldwide system of coaling stations such as Aden. Until well into the 20th century coal was the only energy source capable of sustaining an advanced industrial and commercial society. Without the railway to transport the enormous amounts of coal required such a society could not have been possible.

Apart from a few collieries which had direct access to a canal or navigable river, and for purely local sale at the pithead, virtually every ton of coal mined (225 million tons in 1900) was carried by rail at some stage. Even the substantial sea-borne trade from South Wales and the North East depended upon rail to get the coal to the shipping point.

Developed initially to serve the coal trade but destined to revolutionise land transport and become the most spectacular and far reaching achievement of 19th century engineering, the railway was itself totally dependent upon coal, indirectly to supply the iron and steel for track, bridges, locomotives and rolling

---

* The first Dunston Power station was opened in 1910.

7

The winding engine at Tanfield Lea colliery. The massive construction is typical of 19th century mechanical engineering.   *Beamish Museum*

stock, and directly for fuel and for much of its freight revenue. Whether, up to about the time of World War I, the coal trade and the railway could have existed without the other (except in a very primitive state) is very unlikely. What is certain is that neither could have developed and prospered as they did - and without them the history of Britain, and indeed rest of the world, would have been very different.

Tanfield Moor colliery at White-le-Head on the Tanfield branch after closure in 1947. It had been the oldest working pit in County Durham, having been sunk by the Earl of Kerry in 1726. A typical railway sleeper fence in the foreground.   *Beamish Museum*

Chapter Two

Early Coal Mining in the North East

Coal has been mined in the North East of England from at least the 12th century when the monks of Tynemouth Priory are recorded as having dug coal from outcrops in the cliff face. Coal is mentioned as the fuel for blacksmiths in Bishop Pudney's 'Boldon Book' of 1180 and the townsmen of Newcastle were given the right to dig coal 'without the walls thereof, in the place called the Castle Field and the Forth' in a charter granted by Henry III in 1239. By this time the seaborne trade in coal from the North East to London was well established and mines close to the navigable waters of the Tyne and Wear were ideally placed to develop and profit by it. The exhaustion of the forests within cartage distance of London, much of it due to charcoal burning for iron smelting, and the consequent shortage of firewood, led to an ever increasing demand for coal. There was a Sea Coal Lane in the City as early as 1226. Attempts to limit the burning of coal such as that by Edward I in 1306 which 'prohibyted the burneing of sea-coale in London and suburbs . . . all persons to make their fires of wood' had little effect. Queen Elizabeth I was another who objected to coal being burnt near her palaces, as she 'findeth hersealfe greately greved and anoyed with the taste and smoke of the sea-cooles'.* Coal burning was more than just an annoyance to royalty. Archaeologists studying skeletons from the graveyard of St Helen-on-the-Walls, a poor industrial parish of medieval York, found evidence of sinus infections in over half the burials. It was suggested that this resulted from severe atmospheric pollution from the huge amounts of sea-coal burnt in the local tannery and forge and the large lime kiln which was built in the 13th century to provide cement for the construction of York Minster.†

By the 14th century an export trade to the continent had been developed as witnessed by a record of a ship returning to Pontoise in France with coal from Newcastle in 1328. By the end of the 16th century London had become dependent upon coal from the North East to maintain its normal life, trade and industry. By far the largest city in Britain, with a population of about half a million in 1650, (Bristol, Norwich and Newcastle, each with about 25,000 were the next largest), the capital had become the prime market for coal carried by sea from the Tyne and Wear.

Coal was essential for iron foundries, metalworking, firing bricks and pottery, glassmaking and brewing. The poorer population were dependent upon the coal-fired ovens of the city's bakeries for the bread which formed their staple food and upon the cookshops which provided cooked meat for those who could afford it. Only the relatively well-to-do could afford to cook their food and heat their houses with wood or coal. The city's dependence upon coal had been made clear during the war with the Netherlands in 1666. With the Dutch fleet on the rampage in the Thames estuary and along the East Coast, the

---

* The situation got no better until well into the 20th century. In 1661 John Evelyn published his *Fumigium or the Inconvenience of the Air and smoke of London dissipated* and no Sherlock Holmes film would look authentic without its London 'Particular'.

† Report in *New Scientist* 11th March, 1995.

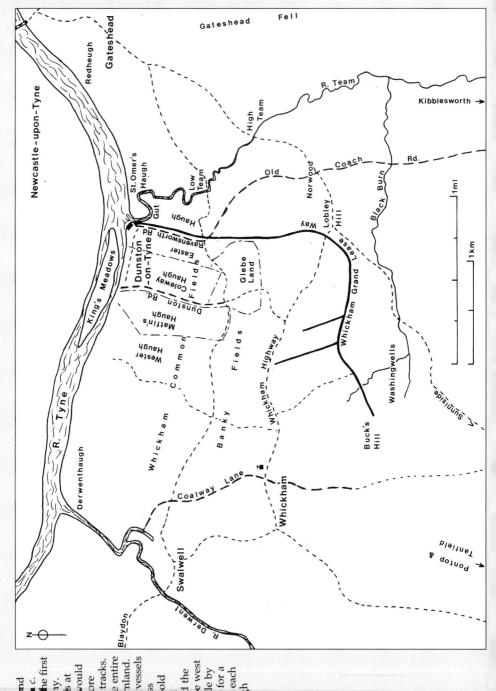

Dunston and Whickham c. 1630 and the first waggonway. Most roads at this time would be little more than farm tracks. Almost the entire area is farmland. Sea-going vessels cannot pass above the old Newcastle Bridge and the Tyne to the west is navigable by keels only for a few hours each side of high water.

Newcastle-upon-Tyne

Gateshead

Gateshead Fell

Redheugh

R. Team

Kibblesworth →

High Team

Coach Rd.

St. Omer's Haugh

Low Team

Old

Norwood

Black Burn

Gut

Haugh

Way

Lobley Hill

1ml

Ravensworth Rd

Dunston-on-Tyne

Easter

Field

Glebe Land

Leases

1km

King's Meadows

Dunston Rd

Coleway Haugh

Whickham Grand

Washingwells

Martin's Haugh

Common

Fields

Wester Haugh

Sunniside

R. Tyne

Whickham

Banky

Whickham Highway

Derwenthaugh

Buck's Hill

Coalway Lane

Whickham

Pontop & Tanfield →

N

Swalwell

Blaydon

R Derwent

colliers were trapped in harbour, raising the possibility that the city would not be able to stock enough coal to survive the following winter when the colliers were normally weather bound in port. The resulting shortage of fuel would have had a severe effect upon the coal-using trades, in particular the bakers - a shortage of bread would have resulted in hunger among the poorer population and probably a good deal of civil unrest. Fortunately the Dutch eventually went home and the coal trade was able to resume in time to supply the market for the winter.

As the demand for coal grew so did the value of the land under which it lay. Pits might be developed by the landowners themselves or licence to mine granted to others on payment of an annual rental and a royalty based on the amount of coal won. The lease of the mines of Whickham and Gateshead, part of the Bishop of Durham's Commons, was granted by Bishop Bury in the 14th century to Sir Thomas Gray and the Rector of Whickham for the substantial annual rental of 500 marks. Queen Elizabeth I, despite her dislike of coal smoke, nevertheless recognised a good investment and in 1582 herself acquired from the Church the 99-year Whickham Grand Lease of the manors and royalties of Whickham and Gateshead at an annual rental of £90. She passed it on to her favourite Robert Dudley, Earl of Leicester, who transferred it to his secretary Sir Thomas Sutton, who in turn sold it in 1584 to the mayor and burgesses of Newcastle for £1,200, an enormous sum at that time and a measure of the value of the right to dig the coal.

Dunston-on-Tyne and Whickham

In that part of the Durham coalfield lying south of the River Tyne and bounded on the east by the broad valley of the River Team and on the west by the narrower valley of the River Derwent lay some of the richest coal seams in the North East (*see map opposite*). The village of Dunston-on-Tyne, now part of the Tyneside conurbation and mainly a dormitory suburb of Newcastle and Gateshead, in the 17th century was a cluster of small dwellings on the south bank of the River Tyne, built on the level Easter and Coleway Haughs* westward from the River Team towards the wetlands along the Tyne bank at the Wester Haugh. The people of the village, numbering perhaps several hundred, were mainly dependent upon farming, the coal trade and the river for their livelihood. There was certainly at least one pub - there were 11 in 1821, the coal trade being a thirsty business!

South-eastwards from Dunston the broad, level valley of the Team stretches some four miles to the village of Kibblesworth. Two miles to the west of Dunston, on the east side of the River Derwent about half a mile from its junction with the Tyne lay the settlement of Swalwell. About half a mile south of the Tyne the side of the valley rises steeply from near sea level to some 400 feet at the ancient village of Whickham which gave its name to the parish. Further to the south and south-west, past the village of Sunniside, the land rises to over 700 feet above sea level to form part of the west Durham plateau centred on Tanfield Moor and Pontop Pike.

* Low-lying, often wetland, close to the river.

At the end of the 16th century the area of land between the present Whickham Highway and the Lobley Hill-Sunniside road was the most productive part of the Great Northern coalfield. The coal was easily accessible, drainage of the pits could be achieved by gravity which also aided the transport of the coal down to the Tyne and its tributaries which, in turn, led to the great and ever expanding London market. No less important, there were men and women, mainly local landowners, with the business flair and ambition for wealth to exploit the situation, and the skilled miners, engineers, waggoners, keelmen and seamen to enable them to do so.

The village of Dunston-on-Tyne in the north-eastern corner of the parish of Whickham has been a focal point for the shipping of coal, carried there by rail, from the early years of the 17th century and throughout the industrial expansion and prosperity of the steam age until the exhaustion of the coal deposits in the mid-20th century ended the trade. In Dunston, coal and the railway were virtually synonymous for almost 350 years and the history of few places can better illustrate the interdependence of the two industries.

Chapter Three

Early Mining Methods and Transport of Coal

The early coal mines were more or less horizontal tunnels (adits) driven into coal outcrops along the valley sides* or simple bell pits. A bell pit consisted of a narrow shaft dug down to the uppermost coal seam; the miners then worked outwards from the bottom of the shaft until contemporary limits of lighting, transport, ventilation and roof support prevented further expansion, when the pit was simply abandoned and another started nearby. The coal was hauled to the surface by horse power, in large baskets (corves), attached to a rope passing over a pulley at the head of the shaft. A single colliery might consist of as many as 30 or 40 of these small pits. As the easily reached uppermost coal seams became exhausted and better methods of underground working were developed, a single, relatively deep shaft could be driven and coal mined at some distance from the bottom of the shaft. A fundamental problem was flooding, particularly in pits in the low-lying valleys. Until this was overcome by Newcomen's steam pumping engine of 1711, the Whickham collieries had an important advantage in that, being situated on high ground, it was a relatively easy matter to connect a number of mines by underground drains which carried the water by gravity to outlets along the valley sides. In some cases an added bonus was that the outflowing water could be used to drive a water wheel which in turn drove pumps to de-water pits lower down in the valley.

Another basic problem was transport. To supply the lucrative London market, coal had to be carried to staiths† on the river banks for loading into sea-going colliers. As the trade increased the pack horses and two-wheeled carts (cowps) used earlier were replaced by wains, large four-wheeled wagons, which, hauled by a team of two horses and two bullocks, could carry close to a ton of coal. The Whickham collieries had another advantage here in that the loaded traffic was largely downhill to the Tyne, the Team and the Derwent. Contemporary roads were not capable of all-weather heavy traffic and numerous complaints and altercations resulted when the waggoners trespassed onto land on either side of the right-of-way in attempts to find better going than the dust bath or deep mud of the 'road'. In winter the wainroads# were usually impassable and despite the spreading of stone to improve the surface and the provision of drainage ditches it might be midsummer before 'the wains were on'.

Wainroads led from the pits at Whickham to storage areas and loading jetties, the staiths, on the Tyne bank at Dunston and on the tidal reaches of the Team and the Derwent (*see map page 10*). Coalway Lane leading from Whickham to Swalwell still defines one of the wainroads and others lay along the present-day Dunston Road and Ravensworth Road.

---

* During the prolonged miners' strike of 1926 some coal was dug from outcrops along the top of the Banky Fields above the Dunston-Swalwell Road.
† An elevated wooden wharf for transfer of coal from waggons into ships or lighters.
# A private right-of-way intended solely for the transport of coal and colliery supplies.

Sea-going vessels, the essential link to the London market, could not pass under the low stone arches of the old Newcastle Bridge and access to the lower Tyne from Whickham by heavily laden wains was barred by the formidable climb from the Team valley over Gateshead Fell. A possible route along the river bank at Gateshead was blocked by the heavily built up area around the Gateshead end of the Tyne bridge. However, for several hours on each side of high tide, small river lighters, the Tyne keels, were able to navigate above bridge to reach Dunston, Derwenthaugh and as far up river as Stella. The Tyne keel was a wooden, clinker-built barge of shallow draught and broad beam; when the wind was favourable it could set a single square sail, but otherwise depended upon the ebb and flow of the tide and the muscles of its crew using long oars (sweeps), one over the side, the other over the stern, to make its way up or down river. Dunston had the obvious advantage of requiring the shortest journey and the low river banks aided loading the keels. The haughs also provided ample level ground for the storage of coal, especially during the winter months when the colliers were laid up by bad weather and coal had to be stored under cover to prevent deterioration by weathering. Below Bridge the coal was loaded by hand into small sailing colliers (pinks) and in later years, the well-known, two-masted, square-rigged East Coast collier brigs which carried the coal to London and the continent.

Between 1600 and 1700 the population of London more than doubled to reach an estimated 600,000. To meet the ever growing demand, and to compensate for the exhaustion of the easily mined coal seams close to navigable water, the industry was forced to open collieries further and further from the rivers with potentially disastrous increases in the already substantial cost and difficulties of transporting the coal to the staiths. It was at this critical time in the early years of the 17th century that the railway, in the form of the horse-drawn waggonway, came on the scene.

The Wayleave System

Coal for export by sea had to be carried from the pits to the nearest navigable water, and although most of the early mines were close to the rivers, this often meant crossing land not owned by the coalowner or lessee. This need for rights-of-way led to the wayleave system, traditional in the North East, in which the colliery owner or lessee paid the owners of the land through which a wainroad or waggonway* passed, an annual rent and a royalty based on the amount of coal passing along the way. This had the advantages of avoiding the expense and often prolonged hassles of obtaining Parliamentary approval for the purchase of land, and avoided the potential loss of the capital cost of purchased land which might be needed for only a relatively short time until the pit was worked out or, as was not unusual, the colliery failed and had to be abandoned. On the other hand, the coal-owner was saddled with an on-going financial drain, which commonly absorbed a significant part of the profits of the colliery and could lead to bankruptcy.

* Waggon and waggonway, spelt with two 'g's was used throughout the waggonway era to identify a vehicle running on rails. This spelling continued in use by the North Eastern Railway into the 20th century.

The cost of wayleaves was often exorbitant. The owners of land hitherto of little monetary worth, on finding that it was proposed as part of a waggonway, would discover that in fact they possessed a piece of real estate of quite impressive value, and would mulct the situation for all they could get. Further, the rental could be raised or the deal cancelled altogether at little or no notice, perhaps due to the machinations of other coal-owners who could also refuse to grant a wayleave to a rival wanting to cross their land. A particularly notorious local character in this respect was William Cotesworth (*c.* 1668-1726), originally a tallow chandler, who worked the system to his own advantage at every opportunity. The Church, a major landowner in County Durham was no less venal when it came to wayleaves - in 1832 the Bishop, Dean and Chapter charged the Stanhope and Tyne Railroad an annual rental of no less than £200 per mile for land near South Shields. In Whickham, the glebe lands of the Rectors were strategically situated between the collieries south of the village and the Tyne at Dunston, a situation which put those reverend gentlemen in a strong position in the matter of negotiating wayleave rents.

The unit used to measure the output of a colliery and the royalty payable for a wayleave was the 'ten', a variable quantity negotiated between the landowner and the lessee and set at so many waggons of an agreed capacity. The tentale, the count of the number of loaded waggons passing along a waggonway, was recorded by tallymen stationed along the way probably using tally sticks, wooden laths in which a notch was cut for each waggon gate (round trip). The capacity of the waggons was measured by the boll or bowle, actually a measure of volume, but equal to about 2.2 hundredweight. In the mid-17th century the usual waggon held about 15 bolls (33 hundredweight) but this was increased over the years until in the late 18th century, the standard became 24 bolls equal to 53 hundredweight or one Newcastle chaldron (fixed by statute in 1695) from which the term chaldron* waggon derived. The ten varied considerably in size. For example on the Bucksnook Way in 1713 it was set at 21 waggons of 19 bolls capacity (about 44 tons) while on the nearby contemporary Stella Grand Lease Way it was 30 waggons of 17 bolls (about 56 tons).

In theory the measured capacity of a waggon assumed that the load was struck off level with the top of the body, but cheating was not uncommon, either by piling the coal well above the waggon sides or, more blatantly, by adding extra planks (greedy boards) to the top of the waggon. Another fruitful source of dispute arose when a wayleave, previously granted for the passage of wains and carts, was assumed rightly or wrongly, to give the right to lay a waggonway.

Negotiating and settling the necessary wayleaves was often as important as engineering factors in determining the route of a waggonway. As may be imagined, endless disagreements, litigation, and often physical mayhem and sometimes outright war were the result. The coal business was well described as 'a fighting trade'.

---

* Just to confuse matters further the London chaldron was only 25½ hundredweight.

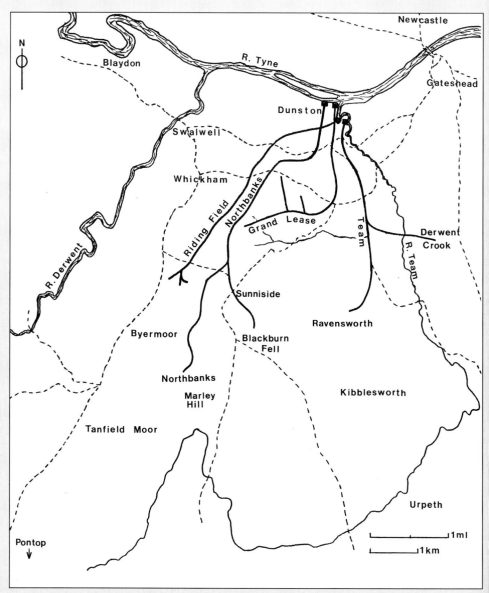

The Coalfield *c.* 1700. Mining is now spreading to the south of Whickham and down the Team valley. Four waggonways have converged on staiths at Dunston. The Team Way follows the earlier Ravensworth wainway along the Old Coach Road.

Chapter Four

The Early Wooden Waggonways

The history of the railway in Britain may be divided into three periods. The first is that of the (usually) wooden-tracked waggonway, horse and gravity operated and lasting from about 1600 until 1825 when the opening of the Stockton and Darlington Railway signalled the second period, that of the steam-hauled public railway running on iron or steel rails. This lasted until the change to diesel traction in the 1960s and the general decline of the railway system.* Although the concept of the railway originated elsewhere, the wooden waggonway was essentially a product of the Great Northern coalfield where it reached its furthest development.

While the practice of laying baulks of timber to facilitate the passage of heavily laden carts over soft ground is very ancient, the critical step of designing a system in which the track also guided the vehicle is first recorded as in use in the metal mines of Bohemia and Austria in medieval times. The idea may have been brought to Britain by German miners employed In the Pennine lead mines in the 15th century. The invention of the flanged wheel which completed the basic concept of the railway seems to have been due to an unrecorded Midlands carpenter, and its first use on a waggonway was by Huntington Beaumont on a two-mile coal-carrying line at Wollaton near Nottingham. Finding his Nottinghamshire mines unprofitable, Beaumont moved to Northumberland where in 1605 he built three waggonways to service his colliery leases near Blyth. His enterprise went unrewarded, probably because he was unable to compete with the powerful consortium of the Newcastle Hostmen which controlled the output (the vend) of the Tyneside collieries, and in 1614 he returned to Nottingham where he died in gaol, bankrupt and embittered.

While the Hostmen no doubt viewed Beaumont's waggonways with interest and his departure with equanimity, they showed no great enthusiasm to apply his ideas to their own collieries. There was no incentive to go to the considerable expense of surveying and laying tracks, building waggons and perhaps negotiating new wayleaves at a time when trade was steady and coal prices moderate and, despite their failings, the wainroads were capable of handling the existing level of traffic.

By the second decade of the 17th century the uppermost coal seams of the Whickham Grand Lease had been worked out and the then lessees (*see map page 10*), led by the Riddells of Gateshead, had been forced to mine the deeper seams to the south of the village. This had been made possible by one of the consortium, Thomas Surtees, who installed a large and expensive system using water-driven pumps to drain the pits. The Lessees sent their coal to the staiths at Swalwell and Dunston by wain, but the Dunston Way had run into difficulties over wayleaves with the Rector and commoners of Whickham who

---

* More recently, electrification of main routes such as the East Coast Main Line and privatisation may perhaps indicate the start of a new era.

17

were demanding higher tolls in view of the greater output from the new pits now passing over their land. To add to their troubles, miners in the Allerdean pit (owned by the Liddells of Ravensworth) allegedly broke into and flooded part of the Lessees' workings. These matters and allegations of rigging the London market were eventually settled after litigation in both the Durham Chancery Court and in the London courts, no doubt to the financial benefit of the lawyers involved. Faced with the need to recuperate their heavy expenditure on developing the new collieries and the subsequent legal costs, the Whickham Lessees looked for a way to raise the efficiency of their operation. They found it in the waggonway.

A wain, pulled by four draught animals could carry 17½ cwt; or at least it could when the wainroads were usable. A waggon running on rails and pulled by only one horse could carry at least twice as much as the wain and do so in all but the most severe winter weather. An added advantage of the waggonway was that on the downhill runs gravity could replace the horse. With the building of the Whickham Grand Lease Way in 1621 the long and profitable partnership of the railway and the coal trade came into being. Beaumont introduced the waggonway to the Great Northern coalfield; it is to the Whickham lessees, Sir Peter Riddell, Henry Maddison, William Hall, Sir Nicholas Tempest and their engineering partner Thomas Surtees, together with the unknown Geordie tradesmen who built and worked the line, that credit must go for establishing the waggonway as a commercial and technical success.

The Whickham Grand Lease Way c. 1621-c. 1705

The Lessees' waggonway to Dunston, the first on Tyneside, was built in about 1621, Surtees probably being the engineer in charge (*see maps pages 10 &16*). From a point to the south of Whickham village the line crossed the head of the northern dene of the Washingwell Woods on a battery (embankment) and continued roughly eastward past Washingwell Farm towards Lobley Hill where it curved round to the north, crossed Whickham Highway and ran downhill to about the Dun Cow Inn and then along or close to the present Ravensworth Road to reach the staiths at the Team Gut. East of Washingwell Farm two short branches extended northward from the main line towards Whickham Highway. By about 1652 the way seems to have been extended westward as far as Buck's Hill. The waggonway proved to be the most successful of the 17th century ways; some years after opening the way the Grand Lease partners had the largest share of the Newcastle vend, amounting to possibly 3,000 tens (roughly 100,000 tons) annually, of which the greater part went down the waggonway to Dunston, the remainder going by wain to Swalwell. The line finally closed some time after 1705.

The Team Way 1669-1964

The Liddells of Ravensworth held the manors of Farnacres, Ravensworth and Lamesley, covering some three miles of the lower Team valley. In 1620 Thomas Liddell had built a wainroad from his pits at Horsemouth Wood on a branch of the Black Burn, to staiths at Dunston (*see map page 16*). Despite the success of the Grand Lease Way and the construction of waggonways elsewhere on Tyneside, the wainway was to serve the Ravensworth mines for some 50 years. The civil war and execution of Charles I and the Puritan regime under Cromwell which followed, had a depressing effect upon the Northern coal trade and inhibited investment in the new technology. As well as the inevitable physical disturbances, many of the coal--owning families were Catholics who supported the Royalist cause and in consequence suffered loss of property and wealth. However, with the political stability following the Restoration of Charles II in 1660, investment in coal trade again became an attractive proposition. Sir Thomas Liddell, having restored some financial stability to his family affairs, now developed an extensive and ambitious drainage scheme using water mills to pump out pits in the Team valley and on the higher ground south and south-east of Ravensworth Castle.

The increased output from the new mines was beyond the capacity of the existing wainroad, and Liddell turned to the waggonway. The early history of the Team Waggonway, built in 1669, is obscure due to the loss of the Ravensworth Estate records, but the route from the colliery east of the castle near Close House Farm was probably along the Old Coach Road to the staith on the Team at Dunston at the northern end of Clockmill Lane. The line, running over slightly undulating ground along the west side of the valley mainly on Ravensworth land, would have had few, if any, problems with wayleaves. In the 1680s a short branch was laid eastward across the Team from a point about 1¼ miles from the staith to a pit at Derwent Crook; this extension survived some years into the 19th century

Traffic on the route was heavy - in 1710 some 120 waggons a day passed over the line, representing over 50,000 tons of coal in a year. In 1717 the way was extended in Ravensworth Park to pits at Robin's Wood (Cocksclose) and shortly afterwards a branch was built extending south to Kibblesworth. Negotiations to extend the line to Urpeth to serve collieries owned by Thomas Bewick ceased when Bewick died and any part of the line which may have been constructed was abandoned. The Kibblesworth branch lasted until about the mid-century. Further development of the Gateshead side of the valley followed in about 1726 with a branch to Allerdene colliery and in the 1760s, another to Eighton.

If the original Old Coach Road route had remained in use, loaded waggons from these collieries east of the Team would have been faced with a climb of some 60 feet up from the bottom of the valley to get to the old way. It is possible that it was in order to avoid this climb that the route was relaid along the valley floor where it remained until modern times. Henry Liddell mentions in 1710 that the way had been improved and this may refer to realignment of the line to its later position. Liddell's original water powered pumping scheme lasted until 1750 when a Newcomen engine was installed at Ravensworth and another at

Norwood 11 years later. A map dated to about 1810 shows a branch leading to the Tanfield Way and the Tyne at Dunston. There seems to have been some redevelopment of the collieries and waggonway about 1839; this may have been a consequence of the upgrading and relaying of the Tanfield branch with iron rails at about that time since the two routes crossed at Team Crossing and were connected, then or later, by a loop line. The further history of the Team Way is described under the later waggonways.

Developments South of Whickham

London's ever increasing demand for sea-coal from the North East could be met only by mining at ever greater distances from the rivers, a situation which the waggonway, fully established by the late 18th century as the best method of transport where the traffic was sufficient to justify the capital costs involved, was well able to meet.

To the south of Whickham to Tanfield, Pontop and beyond there was coal to be won in abundance. To carry it to the Tyne there were three possible routes. To the east lay the Team valley, fully occupied by the Liddells. To the west the Derwent valley offered a route to Derwenthaugh and Swalwell but the valley sides were steep and difficult territory for waggons, and the keels had to navigate an extra two miles beyond Dunston to reach the staiths. In addition the major landowner along the Derwent was Sir James Clavering (1619-1702) of Axwell ('old' Axwell, on the east side of the Derwent), an astute business man who throughout his life remained adamantly opposed to the waggonway. Having made his considerable fortune out of the use of wains alone he saw no need to change his ways. A third route to the Tyne lay down the middle as it were, to either the Derwent or the Team.

The Riding Field Way c.1684-c.1745

Built in about 1684, this waggonway served the collieries of a number of leaseholders with pits on land owned by the Hardings at Riding Field south of Whickham and just to the west of Sunniside (see maps pages 16 & 22). The line ran roughly north-east through the present village of Whickham, down the steep run of the Banky Fields, past Whickham Thorns and over Matfin's Haugh and the Coleway Haugh to staiths on the Team about 250 yards from its mouth. That the partners chose the extra mile to Dunston rather than the shorter western route to the Derwent may have been to avoid the congestion at the Swalwell staiths and the possibility of becoming entangled with and beholden to the Claverings. In 1716 and 1724 shares in both the colliery and the waggonway were acquired by the Montagus and transferred to the Grand Allies in 1726. The Hardings finally sold out to Bowes in 1730 and the line closed in about 1744.

it was cast in bronze and irrevocable. Sir Francis Clavering was still in need of money and he now leased all the Axwell collieries, wayleaves and waggonways to the Allies for a substantial rent. It appeared that the Allies had succeeded where the Coal Office had failed and put Lady Jane out of business. They should have known better.

Thinking that they had the western collieries at their mercy, they first prevailed upon George Pitt, owner of Tanfield Moor, to become an associate of the Allies (he was not apparently of sufficient status to become a full partner) and connect his colliery to the Tanfield Way and buy staith rooms at Dunston. The next step was to dispose of Lady Clavering's coal. They made her several derisory offers to either lease her pits or allow her to win the coal herself and buy it off her. She was not to be had. Her answer was to build her own waggonway. While such a possibility must have been obvious to the Allies there was little that they could do to prevent it short of a trade war, a move for which at that time they lacked sufficient output.

The Tanfield Way 1724-1965

The Allies' new Tanfield Way was to become the best known and one of the longest lasting of the Tyne waggonways (*see map page 22*). The way was opened from Blackburn to the staiths at Dunston and Redheugh in 1724. The route lay past Fugar Bar and then slightly to the north of the Black Burn to reach the old route of the Whickham Grand Lease Way which it followed across Lobley hill and in doing so, avoided the Whickham Glebe and the demands of the Rector. At the top of Lobley Hill at 'the partings' the line divided, one branch going north-eastward to Liddell's staiths at Redheugh while the other went northward past Cowheel (the Dun Cow Inn) and across the Coleway Haugh where it again divided, this time into three branches serving the staiths of the other partners. Pitt's staith was on the Tyne bank just west of the Team mouth, with Bowes' and Montagu's a short distance further upstream. The Redheugh branch and staith were later abandoned and are not shown on a map dated 1787.

By 1725 the way had been extended south to Causey where it twice had to cross the head waters of the Team, here called the Causey Burn. The first crossing, on the main line, was by a massive earth battery (embankment) 100 feet high and 300 feet wide at the base, with the burn confined to a carefully engineered culvert beneath it. The second crossing which carried a branch line to Causey and Beckley collieries was by means of the well-known Causey Arch, built in 1727 by the stone mason Ralph Wood to replace an earlier bridge which had collapsed. The single stone arch, now fortunately preserved after many years of neglect, has a span of 105 feet with the deck, wide enough for double track, about 80 feet above the burn. For their day both the bridge and the embankment were massive and expensive works of civil engineering and rightly regarded as wonders of the age. The Causey Arch was a costly structure when considered as simply part of a branch line but this was a case of spending money to make money. The Allies had coal in the ground in plenty but heavy expenses and it would necessarily be some years before their new pits came into

The massively constructed culvert which takes the Causey Burn beneath the great embankment carrying the Tanfield Waggonway and, nowadays, the Sunniside-Stanley Road. *Author*

The Causey Arch which carried a branch of the Tanfield Waggonway over the Causey Burn. This shows the Arch in its neglected condition before it was recently restored. *Beamish Museum*

The Causey Arch now restored. The scale of the work is best appreciated in this view from
below.   *Author*

full production. The Arch gave access to the leased collieries of Clavering's Beckley and Dawson's Tanfield, both capable of providing immediate and substantial income to tide them over the lean years.

From the Causey Arch crossing several sub-branches spread out to the south-east. The longest reached as far as Tantobie, while another led directly to Dawson's Tanfield near Tanfield Hall and two short offshoots went north towards Beckley. The connection to Beckley has a confusing history, the colliery having been shuttled back and forth between the Tanfield and the Western Way several times. Eventually it settled, together with the nearby Andrew's House colliery (in 1748), as part of the Tanfield system. The Causey Arch became disused some time about 1780 when new branches were laid to Beckley and Andrew's House.

The Tanfield Moor branch built in 1728 left the main line at Bowes Bridge, gave rise to sub-branches to serve Beckley and Northbanks, and then continued westward through Crookgate to reach George Pitt's colliery at Tanfield Moor. The Allies saw this route as a spring board for a future incursion into the western collieries which lay beyond Pickering Nook to the south. However any extension in this direction was scotched by Lady Clavering who had purchased the Lordship of Tanfield Moor and now demanded tentale from Pitt for the use of her land. Pitt took the matter to court, pleading the old excuse that an earlier wayleave for wains allowed the subsequent use of waggons. This failed and with it any hope the Allies may have had of getting the western coal.

From a point on the main line a little to the north of Causey a short branch, the Park Waggonway, went south-east to two pits at Coppy Wood. Further branches eventually covered much of the Tanfield/Pontop area. The earliest, which had been built in 1724 before the main line as part of Montagu's short-lived Blackburn Way led from the Blackburn colliery to Burdon Moor and on to the Bowes land at Hedley Fell. The main line was extended in 1725 to serve Montagu's leases in Causey and Tanfield and was later continued to Shield Row and Oxhill. In 1759 an offshoot was laid to Beamish South Moor (Bowes) and Stanley.

The Tanfield way carried a very heavy traffic, amounting in Lewis's estimation to 930 waggons a day in 1727, carrying something over 2,000 tons of coal. A French visitor Gabriel Jars, described it as 'almost always covered with waggons'. By 1728 conditions on the busiest section had become so congested that a second main way was laid alongside the existing main and bye ways from Bowes Bridge to the 'partings' at the top of Lobley Hill, the only example of a three-track waggonway to be built.

The Third Western Way 1728–c. 1800

The new way was built by a consortium of Lady Clavering, Richard Ridley and John Simpson (*see map page 22*). From Burnopfield the line descended a fearsome 'run' from Bryan's Leap down Busty Bank, which despite very substantial and expensive earthworks, had a gradient of near 1 in 10 and was always the most difficult part of the line to work. The line crossed the Derwent by a stone-arch bridge which was second only to the Causey Arch as an engineering achievement of its day. The rest of the route to the Tyne at Derwenthaugh was on level ground along the west bank of the Derwent, safe from the clutches of the Allies and presenting no problems of construction or operation.

At the northern end of the line a branch, the Lands Way dating from 1728, was laid from a junction at Hagg Hill to serve Albert Silvertop's wine at Norman's Riding. To the south of Burnopfield a complex system of branches extended out to Collierley, Bushblades, Pontop Pike and the Pont Valley. This last branch to Pont Head colliery extended 9½ miles from the staith, the longest distance reached by any of the old wooden ways.

Following the closure of the way south of Winlaton in about 1800 the northernmost section became part of the Garesfield Way, opened in 1801 to serve a pit at High Thornley and later, in 1837, extended to High Spen. In 1889 the line became the property of the Consett Iron Company which extended the way to Chopwell. Apart from upgrading and some realignment, the way, including the stretch of the old Western Way from Hagg Hill to Derwenthaugh, remained in use until Chopwell colliery and the section of the line from Chopwell to Winlaton were closed in February 1961.

The Results of the War

With the completion of the Tanfield and Western Ways the Tanfield / Pontop coalfield was fully occupied by the two lines, which with their widespread networks of branches, made the area safe from any outside invader. The Second Western Way was closed in 1726, the Bucksnook in 1732 and the Riding Field Way, which had been acquired by Bowes was abandoned in about 1745. The 'war of the waggonways', apart from a few last skirmishes, finally petered out. It had been fought to gain control of the coalfield; the means of control was the waggonway; the decisive weapon, the key which opened (or closed) the waggonways, was the wayleave. What had it all achieved?

From the commercial aspect it proved the falsity of Liddell's economic theory - coal prices on the London market on the whole remained stable despite a steady increase both in output and the amount shipped. His attempts to establish a monopoly were in fact bound to fail. The Grand Allies never had output large enough to shut the Western partners out of the market and in any event, before the low-lying pits elsewhere on Tyneside could be adequately drained, the Tanfield / Pontop area was the only part of the coal field capable of large scale production and had therefore a natural monopoly of the trade.

A vast amount of money had been spent on litigation; a great deal of production had been lost, some by legal or semi-legal manoeuvering, some by outright vandalism, all to no profit except to the lawyers.

On a human level the war introduced us to a pair of fascinating characters neither of which would be out of place in a Catherine Cookson novel. William Cotesworth, playing the villain, was a worthy forerunner of those 19th century speculators who saw the railway merely as a counter in the Great Game of

Making Money. Lady Jane Clavering of course was the heroine; she died in 1735, wealthy and respected. All of Cotesworth's schemes and machinations had done little more than cause some temporary upset to her business. She had defied Liddell's Coal Office and exposed the fallacy of its economic theory and successfully defended her territory from the Grand Allies. A canny lass! - she understood the workings of the coal trade better than any of them.

However the effects of the 'war' on the technical development of the railway were, in the long run, more important. By 1700 the waggonway had been accepted as by far the best way to move coal overland in large amounts. By 1730 it had been established beyond any doubt that the waggonway was as vital as the mineshaft itself in winning the coal and a pit of any size without access to a waggonway unless next to navigable water* was virtually unthinkable. The following two centuries would see the map of the Northumberland and Durham coalfield covered by a cat's cradle of waggonways leading to the rivers and the coastal ports. Coal and the railway, until the advent of the public railway in 1825, were in fact, one and the same industry.

In civil engineering the waggonway builders' bridges, cuts and batteries, some on a massive scale, had shown the practicality and developed the techniques of laying a level or reasonably graded road through difficult country.

Their system of track construction of a pair of edge rails connected by transverse sleepers bedded on a layer of ballast for drainage and to spread the load, with the whole based on a firm, well-drained and graded roadbed remains basically that of the modern railway. Even the usually negative effects of abuse of the wayleave system may have had some beneficial results. By forcing the waggonway builders to drive their lines across difficult country such as the descent of Busty Bank on the Third Western Way which they would otherwise have avoided, the improvement of contemporary methods of civil engineering may well have been more rapid than would have otherwise been the case.

The Tanfield and the Third Western Ways were built to the highest engineering standards of their day and represented probably close to the ultimate development of the gravity and horse-drawn, wooden way. These and the other waggonways in the North East attracted the interest of engineers and scientists in both Britain and the Continent; in modern tourism terms they became 'well worth a visit', especially the Causey Arch which deservedly achieved a considerable degree of fame. Some of these visitors published valuable descriptions of their travels, and one, the Frenchman Gabriel Jars, has left accurate scale drawings of waggons and track.

That the Tanfield line required the unique building of a second main way over the busiest section shows that the level of traffic on this line was more than the one waggon/one horse/one man system could cope with on a single track. Any significant increase in carrying capacity and productivity would depend upon improvements in track, waggons and motive power.

It has long been typical of successful commercial and industrial families in Britain that, as their wealth increased, they moved up the social scale and

---

* Collieries close to a river did not necessarily use water transport. Both Dunston colliery and Elswick directly opposite on the Newcastle side of the Tyne (they were connected underground) used rail. Elswick was joined to its own staith by a 'main line' some 230 yards long!

attracted by the delights and cachet of London Society and politics, tended to become increasingly distanced from their business origins. Their sons were sent to Public Schools and read Caesar and Ovid; in Germany their contemporaries studied science, engineering and accountancy! In Britain, particularly in Victorian times, 'Trade' (but not the money it produced) was looked down on. So it was in the Northern coalfield, and the industry was increasingly left in the competent hands of a growing class of professional managers and engineers. Pits were now sunk and waggonways laid out or abandoned more in accord with commercial sense and engineering factors rather than the rivalries of coal politics; there was perhaps less excitement but certainly greater stability and more profit.

Jane Clavering's daughter Alice had married Lord Windsor and although normally resident in London, unlike many of her contemporaries she continued, together with her local partner John Simpson, to run her coal business with as much skill and determination as her formidable mother and the Western collieries and waggonway became dominated by the Windsor/Simpson partnership. One 'invader', George Silvertop of Blaydon, did manage to break into the coalfield when he took a lease of Bushblades and then opened a colliery at Pontop. By the mid-century the four largest collieries on Tyneside were Windsor and Simpson's Pontop, the Allies' Longbenton and South Moor, and Silvertop's Pontop. By 1776 the Tanfield Way had lost its dominance over the Western Way which now had the greater traffic. It was probably at about this time that the Redheugh staith and branch of the Tanfield Way were abandoned. The Clavering and Montagu interests were combined when Alice Windsor's daughter married the 4th Earl (later Marquess) of Bute. When a wayleave for the Western Way became due for renewal, the Marquess as an hereditary Grand Ally (he was a grandson of Edward Wortley Montagu), decided to send his coal down the Tanfield Way to Dunston. The Simpson trustees who had managed the Western Way after the death of John Simpson soon followed suit as did Silvertop and both the Pontop collieries now led to Dunston. By 1800 the Third Western Way had closed apart from the northernmost section which later became part of the Chopwell and Garesfield line and by 1830 the collieries south of White-le-Head had gone leaving the Tanfield and the old Team Way leading to Dunston as the only waggonways in the area.

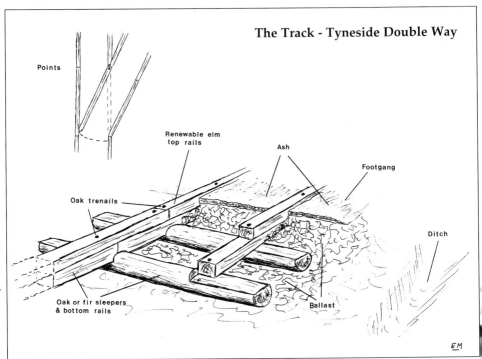

The Track - Tyneside Double Way

Points

Renewable elm
top rails

Ash

Footgang

Oak trenails

Ditch

Oak or fir sleepers
& bottom rails

Ballast

EM

A replica of an early type of wooden-wheeled chaldron waggon standing on wooden track. Its capacity would be about 15 bolls, 33 hundredweight. This view shows the rear ('uphill') end of the waggon with the hefty brake lever (the convoy) acting only on the near side back wheel. The waggon is alongside the Tanfield Railway next to the Causey Arch.   *Author*

Chapter Six

Waggonway Construction and Operation

At a time before iron had come into widespread use and wood, stone and brick were the chief raw materials of construction, the wooden waggonway was one of the great engineering achievements of its day, and the first major advance in land transport since the invention of the wheel.

Determining the route of a waggonway required consideration of both commercial and engineering factors - the availability and very considerable cost, both initial and ongoing, of wayleaves and construction had to be balanced against the expected (or hoped for) traffic and the limits of contemporary technology. The ideal was a steady down gradient for the loaded waggons to make the best use of gravity, but at the same time avoid gradients greater than the accepted maximum of about 1 in 10 and minimise the need for expensive bridges, cuts and batteries (cuttings and embankments); the great embankment and bridge at Causey on the Tanfield Way were exceptional.

Track

The basis of the waggonway and the reason for its success was the track. The rails provided a smooth, level and firm running surface affected only by the most severe weather; the rails, sleepers and ballast together spread the weight of the waggons so that despite heavy loads, the way remained stable even over soft ground. The ballast and drainage ditches ensured that the way never became water-logged. The early ways, and later lines on which the traffic was light, were generally single track with passing loops (bye ways) at intervals but the heavily used ways such as the Tanfield were double tracked with a main way which carried the loaded waggons and a bye way for returning traffic throughout their length. The bye way might be laid to a lighter standard of construction than the main way. There was no standard gauge at this time but on Tyneside the rails were generally laid about 4 feet apart. In his description of the waggonways, the French engineer Gabriel Jars measured the track gauge as *quatre pieds*, i.e. four feet. However as pointed out by Bennett *et al.* Jars was using the French *pied royal* approximately equal to about 12¾ inches making the actual track gauge to be a little over 4 feet 3 inches.

Rails were usually of fir, about 4 inches by 6 in section and 6 feet long, pinned by wooden trenails to oak or ash sleepers. Particularly on the heavily loaded main ways the Tyneside double way was common; this consisted of a second rail of beechwood pinned on top of the fir rail; by wearing to a smooth polish the beechwood gave a both a good running surface and made it possible to replace a worn-out top rail without lifting and relaying the whole track. Sleepers were about 6 inches across and 6 feet long, laid at intervals of 1 foot 6 inches to 2 feet on a layer of ballast which was packed tightly under the rails to carry some of the load. Ballast was usually stone from discarded ship's ballast which was available from incoming colliers in unlimited quantities,

Later chaldron waggons (ex-Londonderry Railway) preserved at Marley Hill on the Tanfield Railway. These are 'standard' 53 cwt waggons with iron wheels, link couplings and more elaborate iron brake gear acting on both wheels on the left side. *Author*

The right-hand side of the same waggons. The latch which releases the bottom door can be seen between the wheels. *Author*

supplemented by furnace clinker, salt-pan ash and sometimes small coal which at that time was of no commercial value. Between the rails the ballast was built up over the sleepers to protect them from the horses' hooves and a layer of sand or boiler ash might be laid on top to give an easier way for the horses and also extended outside the rails as a footgang for the waggoners. The rails were not bent on curves which were laid out as a series of short tangents often with wooden false rails (check rails) pinned to the outside edge of the outer rail. At places such as the staiths where sharp changes of direction were unavoidable, turnrails (small turntables) were used.

Iron rails, first manufactured by the Shropshire ironmasters, were available from 1797, but despite their considerable advantages over wood of longer life and lower rolling resistance, were only slowly adopted on Tyneside, perhaps due to the scarcity of any large scale iron making facilities in the North East at that time. Sometimes iron strips were fastened to the running surface of wooden rails to reduce the rate of wear.

The discovery in 1994/95 of a section of wooden waggonway track complete with a set of points, part of the Lambton Way, at Fencehouses, has given us a true indication of the appearance and construction of the old wooden way.

Waggons

The waggons were built of wood with iron fastenings, with the body carried on two massive longitudinal wooden frames (sole bars). The unsprung wheels, were fixed on iron axles which ran in plain tallow-greased bearings fastened under the sole bars. Originally the wheels were of wood but later the front pair, usually of greater diameter than the rear set, were made of iron. The larger wheels at the front of the waggon were believed to make the draught easier. A simple lever brake (the convoy) applied a massive wooden brake block, usually only on the left rear wheel; wooden wheels were retained on the rear set as they were considered to give better friction for braking. The waggons were never turned for the return trip, the front was always the end facing the staith. An improvement to the convoy believed to have been first used at Shield Row colliery, applied brake blocks to both sets of wheels and the 'long brake' invented in 1795 by a waggoner named Hall at Pontop, enabled a train of waggons to be controlled by one man by arranging for the tension in the couplings to apply the brakes along the train when the waggoner applied the brake on the rear waggon.

Two types of waggon body were common. One had vertical sides and rear with the front end sloping outwards, the other was made with both sides and ends tapering inward towards the sole bars. Unloading was by means of a drop door under the waggon body hinged on the left side and released by a hasp between the wheels on the right. These waggons were the ancestor of the modern high capacity, air-braked, roller-bearing hopper wagon.

In the mid-17th century the common waggon held about 15 bolls, about 33 hundredweight but this was increased over the years until, in the late 18th century, the standard was set at 24 bolls equal to 53 hundredweight or one Newcastle chaldron (fixed by statute in 1695), from which the term chaldron waggon derived.

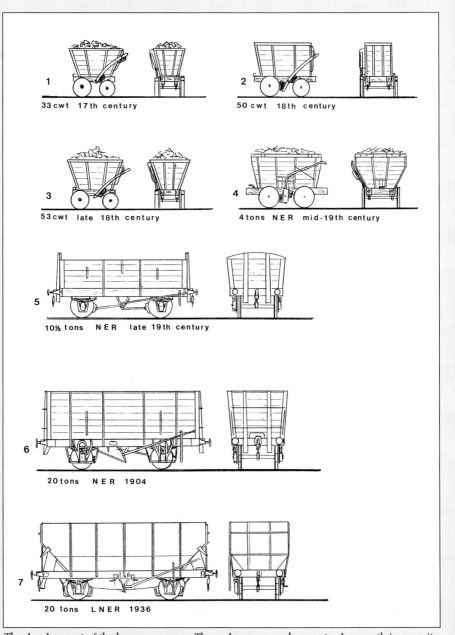

1   33 cwt   17th century

2   50 cwt   18th century

3   53 cwt   late 18th century

4   4 tons   N E R   mid-19th century

5   10½ tons   N E R   late 19th century

6   20 tons   N E R   1904

7   20 tons   L N E R   1936

The development of the hopper waggon. The early waggons show a steady growth in capacity while retaining the traditional style with wooden or later, iron wheels. The 4 ton NER waggon is a transitional type modified for locomotive haulage with dumb buffers and link and pin couplings. Nos. 5 and 6 are larger still, fitted with sprung axle boxes, sprung buffers and chain link couplings but still having end stanchions extended to match the dumb buffers on the old chaldron waggons. Despite their external appearance the internal structure of these waggons was similar to the older types and narrowed towards the bottom doors. The LNER wagon is essentially the NER 20 ton type built in steel in place of wood. It retains the archaic loose couplings and is without continuous brakes.

Operation

The motive power of the early waggonways was supplied by gravity and, on level and uphill stretches, the horse. The horse hauled the waggon by means of traces, the waggon being guided by the rails there was no need for shafts as on a road vehicle. An important accessory was the feed bag, the hay poke; a wisp of hay was often held in front of the horse to encourage it on the upward 'pulls'. The horses usually worked hardest when pulling the empty waggons on the uphill stretches of the bye way back to the pits. On the Tanfield Way where the horses had to drag the loaded waggons a mile uphill to Bowes Bridge on a 1 in 57 gradient, and on the steeper stretches of the bye way, an extra horse was often used, a practice known as marrowing. It was fortunate for the success of the waggonway before the arrival of steam power that, in the Durham coalfield, the loaded waggons were almost always travelling either downhill or on more or less level track. On downhill stretches the horse was detached and trotted behind the waggon on a leading rope, while the waggoner controlled the rate of descent with the convoy. A standard chaldron waggon weighed when loaded about 3½ tons and maintaining control of such a weight on a 1 in 12 gradient with a primitive handbrake must have been somewhat hazardous. Nevertheless contemporary illustrations usually show the waggoner perched on the end of the convoy, nonchalantly smoking his pipe while the horse ambles along behind. One print shows a waggon on either the Whickham Grand Lease Way or the Northbanks Way about to descend down to Dunston - the waggoner is perched on the back and holding down the convoy but there is no sign of the horse which suggests (if this is not just the artist's mistake, he has also drawn wheels without flanges) that the horses may have been led separately down the steeper runs. This would avoid injury to the animal if the waggon ran out of control ('ran amain'), a by no means rare occurrence; the horse was a capital expense to replace, the waggoner presumably had to chance his luck! In wet weather ashes were spread on the rails to improve adhesion but snow and ice could close the way,

> All the ground is covered with snow
> Pit lie idle, pit lie idle

While coal was by far the main commodity carried, ballast, timber for pit props and the ways, and fodder for the animals were also carried as necessary. In the mid-18th century the Tanfield Way carried lead from Shield Row to Dunston. While the waggonways were purely mineral lines, it was no doubt possible to hitch a ride from a friendly waggoner on occasion.

Staiths

Originally the term staith included, in addition to the wooden jetties and coal chutes, extensive undercover storage to prevent deterioration of the coal by weathering. This allowed the collieries to go on working as far as possible, when bad weather in the North Sea prevented the colliers from sailing, and when they were normally laid up in port during the winter and spring. The wealthier London customers seem to have remarkably well informed as to the quality of coal from the various collieries, and coal which had been exposed to the weather could lead to some sharp complaints.

Small and broken coal had little or no commercial value and the early method of loading the keels by simply dumping the coal down a chute tended to cause much breakage and reduced its saleability and in later years a more elaborate method, the 'coal drop', was devised. The waggon was pushed onto a platform suspended at the top of a counterbalanced arm which was then lowered slowly until the waggon was just above the keel. The waggoner, who rode on the platform with his waggon, then opened the bottom door and dropped the load into the keel and the counter-weight lifted the empty waggon back to the top of the staith. The speed of the operation was controlled by a brakeman on the staith.

The history of the early wooden waggonways of the Dunston/Whickham/ Tanfield/Pontop area illustrates the progressive development of the railway, from its adoption in place of the wainroad to the great engineering and commercial achievements of the Tanfield and Third Western Ways. By the end of the 18th century in Britain, the wooden waggonway worked by gravity and horse haulage had evolved into an efficient system of land transport for the coal trade which had both called it into being and nurtured its development from crude beginnings to become a significant engineering discipline in its own right. The ways were designed and built, not by some of the great names in engineering but by local craftsmen, in the phrase used by the 17th century diarist Samuel Pepys writing of the contemporary shipwrights, men whose skill and ability, 'lay confusedly in their hands'. It is regrettable that too often not even the names of these men, the Geordie stonemasons, carpenters, waggonwrights, waywrights and blacksmiths who determined the basic form of the railway, have been recorded.

The waggonway established the flanged wheel, the edge rail and the basic methods of track construction. When the steam locomotive engine entered the picture the road for it to run on was ready.

The steam locomotive did make an early but brief appearance near Dunston. Christopher Blackett of Wylam had been impressed by Richard Trevithick's Pen-y-Darran locomotive, and in 1804 ordered an improved version for his Wylam waggonway. This was built by Trevithick's northern agent John Whinfield at his Pipewellgate foundry on the Tyne bank about 1¼ miles east of the Team mouth. The engine was completed and demonstrated to the 'quality' but was never delivered to Wylam apparently because its 4½ ton weight was considered to be too heavy for the wooden track, and it finished its days as a stationary boiler at the foundry. It was to be over 30 years before the steam locomotive appeared at Dunston.

Chapter Seven

The Newcastle and Carlisle Railway

From about the mid-18th century, an extensive network of canals and turnpike roads had given much of Britain a transport system better than any in Europe. By the end of the century this system had reached close to the commercial and technical limits imposed by the strength, speed and endurance of the horse, the only motive power available.

In view of the success of canals elsewhere in Britain it is not surprising that various schemes for a canal between Newcastle and Carlisle should have been proposed around the end of the 18th century. In 1803 a canal up the Team valley to Beamish was suggested and strongly supported, but the North East remained one of the few parts of the country where the canal never flourished. What is perhaps surprising is that in a region such as Tyneside where the waggonway had thrived for some 200 years the possibility of developing it as a general public carrier seems to have only slowly taken hold. Until now the waggonway had existed and been operated entirely for the use and benefit of the coal trade. By the second decade of the 19th century, Hedley at Wylam and George Stephenson at Killingworth, building on the earlier work of Trevithick and Blenkinsop, had developed the steam locomotive into the practical and reliable machine which was needed to convert the waggonway into the modern railway. However it was not until 1825, when no doubt stimulated by the opening of the Stockton and Darlington Railway (conceived originally mainly as a coal carrying line), that investors accepted as a viable proposition the idea of a public railway between Newcastle and Carlisle. Despite some opposition the promoters pushed ahead and on 22nd May, 1829, by Act of Parliament, the Newcastle and Carlisle Railway Company (N&CR) came into being (*see map overleaf*). Work started the following year and in November 1834 the Blaydon to Hexham portion along the south bank of the Tyne was opened for goods traffic with passenger services following in March 1835. One major problem remained - whether to cross the Tyne to reach Newcastle by a high level bridge at Redheugh or by a low level bridge at Scotswood.

Meanwhile, in 1834, the Blaydon, Gateshead and Hebburn Railway (BG&HR) had come into existence. A clause in the BG&HR Act gave the N&CR company, subject to agreement, the right to construct any part of the Hebburn line between Blaydon and Redheugh. At first there was some dispute over the interpretation of this clause but eventually it was decided to divide the section between them. The BG&HR finally started on the earthworks, if such they could be called, on the level stretch of the Tyne bank through Dunston. As it turned out, this was to be the company's sole achievement.

In 1835 the brothers John and Robert Brandling, members of an old coal trade dynasty, proposed a line, the Brandling Junction Railway (BJR) which would follow much the same route as the BG&HR and obviously compete with it. When yet another company, the Gateshead, South Shields and Monkwearmouth, entered the fray, the Hebburn company lost heart and

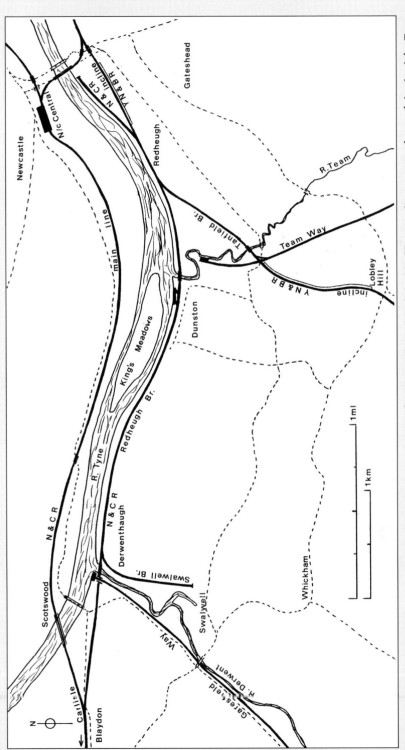

The arrival of the public railways – the Team/Derwent area in 1850. The Newcastle and Carlisle (N&CR) main line runs on the north bank of the Tyne crossing the river at Scotswood. The Newcastle and Carlisle (N&CR) main line runs on the north bank of the Tyne crossing the river at Scotswood. The Redheugh branch from Blaydon lies along the south bank through Dunston to Redheugh where it connects with the Tanfield branch and the Redheugh incline, originally owned by the Brandling company but now belonging to the York, Newcastle & Berwick (YN&BR), soon to become part of the North Eastern Railway. Of the old waggonways, only the Tanfield (now the Tanfield branch), the Team and the Garesfield (on the route of the Third Western Way) remain.

disappeared leaving the N&CR to take over the Dunston section and complete the line through to a temporary terminus on the Tyne bank at Redheugh. The Blaydon to Derwenthaugh section opened on 11th June, 1836 and the further section to Redheugh followed on 1st March, 1837, with a ferry service across the Tyne from the Redheugh quay to connect with the company's wharf and station at the Close in Newcastle.

The expense of bridging the Tyne at Redheugh proving to be prohibitive, the company reverted to the original scheme of a low level bridge at Scotswood. The line along the north bank reached a temporary terminus at the Shot Tower in 1839 and was extended to the Forth in 1847 before finally reaching Newcastle Central on 1st January, 1851. With the completion of the route north of the river to the Shot Tower in 1839, the line through Dunston was reduced in status to become the Redheugh branch. Before that however the Newcastle and Carlisle Railway Company had celebrated the completion its main line with the grandest of Grand Opening Ceremonies on 18th June, 1838. It was an occasion typical of such affairs in 19th century Britain, graced with the 'quality' in their finery and the 'commonalty' in their thousands, dignified by civic pomp, aldermanic orations, brass bands and cold collations, but which unfortunately degenerated into chaos and confusion.

Five trains left Carlisle at 6 am for Redheugh where, while boarding the ferry, some of the guests were accidentally deposited in the coaly Tyne, fortunately with nothing worse than dampness and loss of dignity. It was an omen of things to come. Inexorably falling behind schedule, some 3,500 passengers filling a caravan of 13 trains totalling 130 'carriages' (many of them open waggons) hauled by all but two of the company's engines with another running ahead as pilot, set out for Carlisle in persistent fog which soon turned to rain. Following the ceremonies at Carlisle, further excessive delays in rearranging the trains delayed the start of the return trip until 10 pm. The procession eventually trundled slowly eastward through darkness, thunder and rain to Redheugh, the last train depositing its cold, wet, bedraggled cargo at 6 am the following morning. It says much for the ability of the train crews that the whole 180 miles of running, much of it in fog, rain and darkness, of a procession of trains with only primitive brakes on a line completely without signals, resulted in only one derailment and two relatively minor accidents to the passengers.

The Redheugh branch, running along the Tyne bank close to the river, was virtually level throughout, the only engineering works of note being the wooden bridges over the Derwent and the Team. The Redheugh quay was convenient for the trans-shipment of goods while passengers had five trains each way daily and three on Sundays, all timed to connect with the main line services at Blaydon. Dunston did not rate a station but trains stopped at Derwenthaugh for Swalwell which was given its own half-mile-long branch from an eastward facing junction at Derwenthaugh opened on 24th May, 1847.

Until the abandonment of the old Tanfield staiths at Dunston, the Redheugh branch passed beneath the staiths' approach tracks with no connection between the lines. In 1838 the N&CR erected its own staiths at Dunston to handle coal brought down the line from pits further up the Tyne valley.

An N&CR train was a handsome affair. Carriages were all four-wheeled, painted yellow with black lining for first class and green with white lining for second class; from about 1843 both classes were painted claret, with black and yellow lining for firsts and white and yellow for seconds. Luggage vans were green. All displayed the coats of arms of Newcastle and Carlisle and carried names such as *Transit* and *Despatch*. Whether they were very comfortable is another matter. Apparently third class passengers had to do with open goods wagons fitted with seats 'as required'. Locomotives were painted a dark red (variously described as brown, Indian red and maroon) with the usual polished brass fittings of the period. Like the carriages they had names, usually of prominent people, *Victoria* and *Collingwood* or local places, *Hexham* and *Alston*. All the company's engines (with one exception, No. 3 from Bury, Curtis & Kennedy of Liverpool) were obtained locally, from Robert Stephenson & Co., Hawthorn & Co., Hawks & Thompson of Gateshead and Thompson Bros of Wylam. All except some early 0-4-0 types were six-wheeled with either four or all six wheels coupled; the company never used the six-wheeled 2-2-2 type with only a single driving axle, popular for express work at that period, probably because speeds were low and the long pull eastwards from Wetheral to Brampton mainly at a gradient of 1 in 107 argued in favour of coupled wheels for better adhesion.

Goods traffic on the Redheugh branch was substantial, the Redheugh quay being particularly convenient for interchange with river-borne traffic, notably lead ore from the Pennine mines and incoming timber (mainly pit props) from the Baltic. The new cross-country route led to a considerable increase in trade between Tyneside and the North West and Ireland and introduced such culinary delights as Irish bacon, hitherto unknown on Tyneside.

While not among the leading railways in Britain with respect to size, the N&CR was a well run and profitable business, paying regular annual dividends of around 5 to 6 per cent throughout its independent existence. However, in view of its position as a small but important and profitable cross-country line it was inevitable that, with the spate of railway amalgamations which occurred in the 1860s, it would sooner or later be absorbed by one of its more powerful neighbours.

Chapter Eight

The Brandling Junction Railway

Work on the Brandling line began in August 1836 directed by the engineer Nicholas Wood, a respected mining and railway engineer and a friend and colleague of George Stephenson. When taking over the BG&HR company's powers the N&CR had made an agreement not to extend the Carlisle line eastward beyond Redheugh into Brandling territory and to make a connection with the Brandling line at a point about 400 yards west of the Redheugh terminus, while the Brandling company agreed to take over the old Tanfield Waggonway which now became the Tanfield branch, and to relay and upgrade it to contemporary standards (*see map page 42*).

The BJR was opened throughout for passenger and goods traffic on 5th September, 1839. From a westward-facing junction at Redheugh the rope-worked Redheugh incline climbed diagonally up the steep side of the Tyne gorge above Pipewellgate at a gradient of 1 in 23 to Oakwellgate, where a 60 horsepower steam winding engine was erected. The incline, which opened for goods traffic on 15th January, 1839, was to have a significant effect upon coal shipments at Dunston. The power of the steam engine had now overcome the barrier presented by Gateshead Fell and so bypassed that other obstruction, the Tyne Bridge (and the keelmen), enabling coal from the Tanfield and Pontop collieries to be carried by rail via the BJR to deep water staiths down river.

The N&CR was unusual among British railways in that, on double track, its trains ran on the right. At Redheugh the BJR trains, running on the left, used a short stretch of the N&CR line between the Redheugh incline and the Tanfield branch which raises the interesting question of how the conflicting traffic was handled at a time when signals and point interlocking were still in the future.

*The Tanfield Branch**

When, in 1825, the original 99-year agreement which created the Grand Allies expired, two of the then partners, the Lords Ravensworth (Thomas Liddell) and Wharncliffe (of the Bute/Montagu family) had little interest in maintaining their connection with the coal trade and attempted to sell their collieries. Failing in this, the agreement was renewed for a further 30 years under the management of Nicholas Wood as their local agent. By this time the Tanfield Way seems to have deteriorated and lost much of its traffic. Marley Hill pit had been closed as uneconomical in 1815 and George Pitt's old line to Burnopfield and Pontop closed at about the same time (*see maps pages 22 & 42*). The Stanhope and Tyne, another route which used the power of the steam engine to tackle gradients impossible for the horse, opened its line in 1834 and had captured the traffic from Tanfield Moor colliery and the pits around Beamish and South Moor which had until now gone down the Tanfield line (*see map page 92*).

* Although officially known as the Tanfield Branch it was always referred to locally as 'the waggonway'.

In February 1839 the BJR began modernising the waggonway between Tanfield Lea and Lobley Hill, still apparently laid with the old style wooden track, using iron rails laid to standard gauge and converting the steeper runs into rope-worked balanced inclines or installing steam winding engines. The branch opened for goods traffic on 26th November, 1839. Having failed to complete the line to Redheugh before the end of 1836, it was forced by previous agreement to compensate the Marquess of Bute for not being able to carry his coal down the new route. The Brandling line was built using the wayleave system and the delay appears to have been due to the seemingly inevitable problems in negotiating rights-of-way. That Bute was the only coal owner to be awarded compensation suggests that his Tanfield Lea colliery was the only one still sending any significant amount of coal to Dunston at that time.

From the foot of the Lobley Hill incline the line was relaid along the route of the long-closed Ravensworth branch to Redheugh, crossing the Team Way on the level at the Team crossing, to join the Redheugh branch of the N&CR. The three existing branches from the top of Lobley Hill to the Tyne at Dunston were abandoned. There were three stationary engine-worked inclines, at Sunniside, Causey Wood West and Causey Wood East, the latter two being worked by the same engine at the summit between the two inclines at Bowes Bridge. In a situation like this, the usual arrangement was for the winding drums for the two inclines to be geared together so that the waggons being lowered down one side helped in part to balance the upward pull. Self-acting (balanced) inclines were installed at Fugar Bank (Baker's Bank) and Lobley Hill. The intervening sections were worked by horses. Gradients on the inclines ranged from 1 in 317 near the top of Causey Wood West to a maximum of 1 in 12 on Fugar Bank. This substantial and expensive rebuilding of a run-down waggonway, apparently to serve a single colliery at Tanfield might seem rather speculative. However considerable developments were in hand on the coal field around Marley Hill. The third partner of the Grand Allies at this time was John Bowes, young, intelligent and hard working, and who, unlike his lordly partners, took a considerable and far-sighted interest in his collieries.

In 1839, with Nicholas Wood as Engineer and partner, he formed the Marley Hill Coal Company and proceeded to sink a new pit at Marley Hill, which was opened in 1840 and joined to the Tanfield line. By 1845 the branch had been extended to new collieries at Crookbank and Burnopfield, and by 1847 Marley Hill alone sent 270,000 tons of coal and coke down the line to Redheugh and beyond. Much of this development was due to the energy and initiative of Charles Palmer, son of the owner of Palmer's saw mill at Dunston, who had joined Bowes as a partner in 1844. It seems obvious that the Brandlings were well aware that these developments were pending (Nicholas Wood was after all, Engineer to both concerns) when they decided to invest in the Tanfield line.

On 18th June, 1842 what has been claimed to be the first branch line passenger service in Britain, was started between Tanfield and Greenes-field [sic] in Gateshead, calling at Bowes Bridge, Fugar Bar and (by request) Lobley Hill. Dunston had to wait another 67 years to get its own passenger station. The service was somewhat primitive, the carriage at first supplied was soon replaced by a coal waggon!

At this time the financial affairs of the BJR were found to be less than sound due to some 'creative accounting' by the Directors, despite which the company continued to expand. In 1840 the Tanfield branch was extended by a rope-worked balanced incline with a maximum gradient of 1 in 15 to recapture the traffic from Tanfield Moor colliery. The line from Tanfield Moor to the Stanhope and Tyne route was closed at this time, but restored in 1843 to connect with the Derwent Iron Company's Consett works and enable lead ore and limestone from the western end of the Stanhope and Tyne to go down the Tanfield branch.

The Brandling Junction route occupied a strategic position greater than its local status might suggest. Not only was its line between Brockley Whins and Gateshead part of the then East Coast route from London, but its line at Gateshead covered the probable site of the southern end of the high level crossing of the Tyne which would inevitably be built in the near future.

George Hudson, a linen draper of York and a far-sighted, enterprising and ruthless businessman, had become deeply involved in railway promotion and was Chairman and leading figure in a number of companies. Hudson had a burning ambition to see the East Coast route from London to the North completed by companies under his control, and in 1844, in a typical Hudson move, he descended upon the Brandling Directors and frightened them into selling their line to him personally at a bargain price. He then transferred the company to his Newcastle and Darlington Junction Railway, not without financial advantage to himself. With the amalgamation of some of the East Coast companies which followed, the Tanfield branch in July 1845 was amalgamated with the Newcastle and Darlington Junction Railway which in August 1847 became part of the York, Newcastle and Berwick Railway. Hudson's financial wheeling and dealing, while often to his own profit, greatly benefited both the shareholders of his various companies and the establishment of the railway system of the North East and the Midlands. However, investigation of his methods revealed, among other matters, that capital funds had been used to inflate dividends, and in 1849 he was forced to resign in disgrace.

With the establishment of the Newcastle and Carlisle and the Brandling companies and the upgrading of the Tanfield Way, the local railway scene had changed dramatically in less than a decade, from the old wooden--tracked, horse-drawn waggonway dedicated to the carriage of coal to the modern, mechanically-powered railway, running on metal rails to a published timetable, carrying passengers and whatever goods and mineral traffic was offered to it. The railway was now an independent business and industry in its own right, still dependent upon coal for its motive power and much of its revenue but no longer simply the servant and prerogative of the coal trade, to which it would nevertheless continue to supply an essential and ever-growing service.

The Pontop and Jarrow Railway

While the Tanfield branch, in 1847 serving seven collieries, depended for its revenue upon the coal traffic, it was owned by a company which was a general carrier and not subject to control by the mine owners. The dependence of the collieries upon the railway company for the supply of waggons and the tendency for the company to operate the line to suit its own needs, together with increasing congestion and delays on the line, led Palmer and Bowes to build their own line eastward from Marley Hill to connect with their existing waggonway from Kibblesworth (acquired in 1851) to the Tyne at Jarrow. This, the Pontop and Jarrow Railway (the Bowes Railway from 1932), was fully opened for traffic in 1855 (*see map page 92*). Coal from the partner's collieries at Marley Hill, Crookbank (1847, replaced by Byermoor in 1860), Burnopfield (1849), Andrew's House (1852) and Dipton (1855) was lost to the Tanfield branch thereby depriving the NER (which came into being in 1854) and now owned the branch, of some £20,000 revenue a year, although a connecting link between the two lines was retained at Bowes Bridge Junction, a little to the north of the point at Marley Hill where the two routes crossed on the level.

The Pontop and Jarrow was a considerable enterprise, having at its greatest extent a main line about 15 miles long from Dipton to the staiths at Jarrow. From the high point on Birk Heads moor about one mile east of Marley Hill, a series of self-acting and stationary engine-worked inclines led across the Team Valley and over Blackham's Hill to Springwell Bank Foot; the eastern and western sections of the line were operated by locomotives although a rope-worked incline remained between Burnopfield and Crookgate until 1900. Locomotives were first used at Marley Hill in about 1847, the section having been earlier worked by horses. The locomotive shed at Marley Hill, built in 1854, is still in use by the preserved Tanfield Railway.

Chapter Nine

The North Eastern Railway

The middle years of the 19th century saw a series of railway company amalgamations which, while not entirely without problems, were to settle the ownership of the public railways in the North East for some 70 years. The major step was the formation of the North Eastern Railway (NER) which came into being on 31st July, 1854 by the amalgamation of the York, Newcastle & Berwick, the York & North Midland and the Leeds Northern railways, occupying between them territory in Northumberland, Durham and the North Riding (North Yorkshire). Thus was Hudson's grand design of an East Coast route between London and the North under one management in part achieved, although by now his enterprising career had ended. Two large companies in the region, the Newcastle and Carlisle and the Stockton and Darlington (S&DR), remained independent, a situation which was to give the NER some trouble.

The Railway that might have been

North of the Border in the 1860s the North British Railway (NBR) was in a mood of aggressive expansion. Having obtained control of the Border Counties line running from the Scottish border down the valley of the North Tyne to Hexham, it now had ambitions of reaching Newcastle via the Carlisle line. To the south-west of the NER territory a proposed South Durham and Lancashire Union Railway across the bleak, high country of Stainmore, would link Tebay in the west with Barnard Castle on the S&DR system in the east. From Barnard Castle a possible route northward led into the heart of the NER territory, passing through Consett with its iron works and then down the Derwent valley to join the N&CR near Swalwell. After some years of political manoeuvring and failed Parliamentary Bills, a Newcastle, Derwent and Weardale scheme was put forward, its proposed route running from Newcastle via Redheugh, Dunston, Swalwell and the Derwent valley to connect with the South Durham and Lancashire, the Stockton and Darlington and the West Hartlepool railways. Behind this scheme were the North British and no less than the 'Premier Line', the mighty London & North Western Railway (LNWR), which latter company had a grudge in that it believed that the NER was treating it unfairly with regard to the interchange of cross-country traffic between East and West.

The proposed line included branches and running powers penetrating deep into the Durham coalfield and into Newcastle Central; the possibility of the LNWR getting its hands on the profitable Durham coal traffic, added to the equally unpleasant prospect of North Western trains passing under the very walls of the NER works (just to the west of the Gateshead end of the High Level Bridge) and into Newcastle Central, spurred the NER to introduce into Parliament its own Bill for a line between Blaydon, Blackhill and Consett along the Derwent valley.

In the end all was settled amicably. With the LNWR satisfied by new arrangements for the interchange of traffic at Carlisle, the NER was able to get Parliamentary approval for its own Derwent valley line from Scotswood Bridge to Blackhill without opposition and the line was opened in 1867 (*see map page 92*). The North British was pacified by being given running rights for its trains between Hexham and Newcastle Central and Redheugh but had to allow the NER to use its own locomotives to haul the prestigious East Coast expresses between Berwick and Edinburgh, which was probably the better bargain. The South Durham and Lancashire Union line was opened in 1861 and transferred to the S&DR the following year. Thus the possibility that Dunston might have been served by the London & North Western and later the London, Midland and Scottish Railway evaporated. The N&CR and the S&DR had by now accepted that their future lay with the NER, with which they amalgamated, the N&CR on 17th July, 1862 and the S&DR on 13th July, 1863. With the exception of the many privately owned colliery lines such as the Team Waggonway and the Pontop and Jarrow Railway, the railways in the region were now united in the single ownership of the North Eastern Railway.

Unlike many contemporary companies, the NER was remarkably successful in defending its territory from competing lines. This, as described above, it usually achieved by amicable arrangements for the transfer of traffic and the exchange of running rights with neighbouring companies. In 1913 the company owned 4,762 miles of track and had an issued share capital of £56,814,000 making it the fourth largest railway company in Britain exceeded in size only by the Great Western (the largest), the Midland and the London & North Western companies. Despite its near monopoly of rail transport in the region, the company seems to have treated its customers, both private and commercial, with a level of fairness and consideration often lacking in many of its contemporaries. The company did however have a strong aversion to running its trains on Sunday; in the summer of 1914 for example, when one might have expected to find a busy excursion traffic, over one third of its route mileage was closed on that day.

The Redheugh branch continued to carry a considerable amount of mixed goods traffic to and from the Carlisle line and the Redheugh quay, while a never ending stream of trains carrying coal from the Tanfield branch and from collieries around Blaydon pounded up the bottleneck of the Redheugh incline, now converted from rope working to locomotive power. The steady growth of industrial concerns around Dunston which followed the opening of the Redheugh branch also contributed their share of business to the railway.

NER Locomotives

The locomotives designed by Edward Fletcher, the first Locomotive Superintendent of the NER were typical products of Victorian railway engineering, rather ornate but of robust and lasting construction. They were distinguished by stove pipe chimneys, bell-mouth domes carrying a pair of Salter spring-balance safety valves, and a round-roofed cab usually with rectangular spectacle glasses. For mineral and general goods traffic the classic British inside cylinder 0-6-0 tender engine was by far the most common type,

NER '1001' class No. 1194. A fine example of a mid-Victorian 'long boiler' goods locomotive designed by William Bouch (until 1863 Engineer of the Stockton & Darlington Railway) and built as No. 194 *Alice* at Shildon in 1866. The photograph is thought to have been taken in about 1874 at Bishop Auckland. At least one of the class ended its days in 1906 at Borough Gardens Shed in Gateshead.   *Rail Archive Stephenson*

with some examples of the Stephenson 'long boiler' 0-6-0 type with all the wheels in front of the firebox which gave a decidedly tail-heavy look to the engine. The hard slog up the Redheugh incline might require as many as three banking engines behind the train to 'shove up' and Fletcher built some massive, outside-framed saddle tanks, the 'incline engines' for this type of work, one being stationed at Gateshead to assist on the Redheugh incline.

T.W. Worsdell who became Locomotive Superintendent in 1875 (followed by his brother Wilson Worsdell in 1880), established what was to be the NER style for the remainder of the company's existence. Compared with Fletcher's designs, Worsdell's engines were plain, almost austere, but well proportioned with handsome boiler fittings and a relatively roomy, side-window cab at a time when most builders provided little more than a windshield and a vestigial roof to shelter the footplate men. While the engines were rather plain they were embellished with a handsome livery of green (varying in shade somewhat depending upon the works which applied it) lined out with black outlined with white and with a broad claret border around the cab sides and tender or tank.* The safety valve cover and the joint ring between the boiler and the smokebox were polished brass and a large oval, brass number plate was carried on the cab.

Wilson Worsdell continued his brother's style of locomotive although he did not persist with some of his engineering features such as compounding and he simplified the engine livery by omitting the claret border as an economy measure. One of his designs which was to work around Dunston almost to the end of steam was the pretty class 'E1' 0-6-0 (LNER 'J72') shunting tank, a development of his brother's class 'E' (LNER 'J71'). These engines were unique in Britain in that the design was not only perpetuated by the LNER but a further batch of 28 was actually built by British Railways; the last survivor was withdrawn in 1964.

* The variations in railway liveries are many and complex. See for example *North Eastern Record* Vol. 2.

NER class 'BTP' (LNER 'G6') was a Fletcher design built in 1874 for light passenger duties. Based at Gateshead Shed, No. 955 as shown in the photograph had been rebuilt with a Worsdell cab, boiler and fittings. This engine worked the Dunston service in the 1920s and it is shown coupled between a pair of clerestory coaches to form an auto-train.

North Road Railway Museum, Darlington

NER class '476' Edward Fletcher's incline engine, built in 1875 at Gateshead, No. 476 worked 'shoving up' on the Redheugh incline until it was withdrawn in 1905.

North Road Railway Museum, Darlington

NER class '398' class, designed by Fletcher and built in 1874 by R. & W. Hawthorn. A typical late Victorian goods engine, No. 984 was finally scrapped from Borough Gardens Shed in 1922.

LCGB/Ken Nunn Collection

NER class 'P1' class (LNER 'J25'). An example of the classic British 0-6-0 tender engine. A Wilson Worsdell design built at Gateshead in 1900, No. 2071 spent World War II on loan to the Great Western Railway and subsequently survived until 1958. Many of the class served on Tyneside, on heavy mineral and goods trains until displaced to lighter duties by the more powerful 'P2', 'P3' and the 0-8-0 engines.

Rail Archive Stephenson

NER Waggons

In the mid-19th century the bulk of the NER coal traffic was still carried in the traditional chaldron waggon but with the capacity raised to four tons and with some necessary modifications to adapt them for locomotive haulage. Both axles, still without springs, were now fitted with cast- or wrought-iron wheels of the same diameter and the wooden sole bars were extended at each end to form dumb buffers and chain link couplings were fitted. A single handbrake lever on one side applied massive wooden or, on later versions, iron brake blocks to both wheels on that side of the waggon. For ease of operation waggons were marshalled on the track with the brake levers on the same side. Waggon bodies were of wood with iron strapping and both sides and ends tapered inwards towards the bottom. Wooden, or sometimes iron, 'batter boards' were attached to the sides and ends of the body; when the coal refused to drop out of the bottom door, particularly in icy weather, a few good clouts on the batter board with a large hammer would get it moving again. From about 1860 the company began to dispose of its large stock of chaldrons, replacing them with more modern hopper waggons of 6 to 8 tons capacity, fitted with springs, grease lubricated axle boxes and standard buffers and three-link couplings. NER locomotives which were used for mineral traffic were fitted with a pair of massive wooden blocks attached to the buffer beam and extending below it to enable the engine to buffer up to the lower, closer-set dumb buffers on the chaldrons.

The collieries themselves acquired chaldron waggons, 'black waggons', so called because they were normally painted with pitch or tar, of 3 or 4 tons capacity generally similar to the NER type and often second-hand NER stock. Many of the smaller waggons were eventually upgraded by fitting 'greedy boards' above the top plank to increase the load to 4 tons. The NER banned the use of dumb-buffered vehicles on its lines in 1913 but large numbers of the old NER chaldron waggons were bought by the collieries where many survived in pit yards and on the private lines well into the mid-20th century, some only being scrapped after being taken over by the National Coal Board in 1947. NER goods and mineral waggons were painted grey with white lettering shaded black. On at least some stock the company name and division* were given in full but over the years the increasing need for economy led to the use of the initials NER only and the black shading was abandoned.

---

* The NER was organised into three divisions, Tyneside being part of the Northern Division.

Chapter Ten

Coal and Industry

Just as the need of the coal trade for heavy transport had fostered the development of the railway, so the necessity of draining water from deep mines promoted the development of the steam pumping engine. As the coal seams near the surface became exhausted attempts to mine the deeper deposits were often thwarted by flooding of the workings by water in amounts far beyond the capacity of any water- or horse-powered lifting or pumping device.

The first practical application of steam power to mine drainage was Thomas Savory's condensation pump in 1698, followed by Thomas Newcomen's atmospheric 'fire engine' first installed in a Staffordshire coal mine in 1711. Newcomen's engines were soon adopted throughout the coalfields and in the tin mines of Cornwall. James Watt produced his more efficient double-acting pumping engine with a separate condenser in 1769, followed in 1781 by the rotative engine which was taken up by the textile mills in place of the water wheel. The relatively meagre appetite for coal of Watt's machines made them particularly popular in Cornwall far from the coalfields, but in the Midlands and North the less efficient atmospheric engine long persisted since it ran well enough on the ample pithead supplies of unsaleable small coal.

With the advent of the steam locomotive, the railway had progressed from its earlier status as an adjunct of the coal trade to become an engineering and commercial entity in its own right. Similarly the stationary steam engine moved from the mine to a multitude of applications in factory, mill, workshop and ship, all fuelled by coal.

The long years of Victoria's reign saw fundamental changes in the social, commercial and industrial structure of Britain due in a large part to the railway. At her accession in 1837, the population of about 18 million was largely rural and, by present day standards, industry was generally restricted to small enterprises of mainly local importance. London was by far the largest city with a population of about two million in 1837. By 1900 London's population had grown to over six million and that of the country as a whole had doubled to 37 million, 80 per cent of which was urban, living in towns and cities which had often been little more than villages when Victoria came to the throne. Industry was now dominated by large joint stock companies with employees numbered in thousands; the railway companies themselves were prime examples. These changes inevitably affected the coal trade.

The coal shipped from the North East to the Thames had for centuries supplied a market of domestic consumers and small tradesmen such as blacksmiths and bakers. As London's population grew the suburbs spread further and further away from the riverside wharfs and coal depots. At the same time the new suburbs found themselves connected by the railways to the coal fields of Yorkshire, Nottinghamshire and South Wales. The small local coal merchant, rather than buying Tyne coal from the Thameside factors who had until now monopolised the trade, could now order his supply directly from his preferred colliery and have it railed in convenient wagon loads to his local station, usually in his own privately-owned wagons. Inevitably the railways, notably the Great Northern, captured much of the domestic market to the detriment of the North Eastern sea-borne trade. By 1880 almost two-thirds of the 10 million tons of coal a year entering London, apart from a relatively insignificant amount coming in by canal, was 'inland', carried entirely by rail.

While the actual tonnage of sea-coal showed little change it represented a decreasing proportion of an increasing market until about 1870 when it began to rise. Fortunately for the North East the growing demands of Thameside industry for coal were to restore and increase the sea-borne trade until by the end of the century it was supplying more than half the capital's annual imports of over 15 million tons.

The steam engine revolutionised transport by sea just as it had done on land. The 19th century sailing collier, carrying 200 to 400 tons of coal could make perhaps 10 round trips between the Tyne and the Thames during the eight or nine months of the year when sailing was possible. The first steam collier, the *John Bowes* built in 1852, appropriately at Palmer's Hebburn yard, could carry twice the load of a sailing collier and make 30 round trips a year, summer and winter. By the end of the century steam colliers were carrying over 1,000 tons a trip, mostly for the bulk supply of Thameside industries.

Because of their appearance the more modern Thames colliers were known as 'flatirons'; to allow them to pass under the Thames bridges they were built with a very low superstructure and masts and funnels which could be temporarily lowered to deck level. Among the greatest users of coal were the gas companies; the great Beckton works of the Gas, Light & Coke Company, for example, imported over one million tons annually, carried in its own fleet of colliers. Other major users of coal were breweries, cement works, paper mills, water and sewage undertakings and the fleets of merchantmen using London's docks and needing bunker fuel. After the turn of the century millions of tons of coal were shipped to the electricity generating stations which now provided electric light and powered increasing numbers of electric motors, the London Underground, the tramway system and many of the suburban train services. Since much of the sea-borne coal supplied to the gas and electricity undertakings still went indirectly to the domestic consumer in the form of light and heat, the loss of this market was less severe than it might appear and the demand for coal from the North East grew steadily, particularly for the highly rated Durham gas and coking coals. As colliery output rose to meet demand, the existing rail and staith facilities became increasingly inadequate and the coal owners began to press for improvements.

Changes had occurred on the Tyne as well as on the Thames. Following the opening in 1876 of the handsome swing bridge, designed by John F. Ure and built by W.G. Armstrong & Co. and the subsequent demolition of the old stone-arch bridge which for so long had isolated the upper reaches of the river, the Tyne Improvement Commission had dredged and deepened the river as far as Derwenthaugh and completely removed the island of King's Meadows. Sea-going colliers could now reach Dunston, a fact which some of the Durham coal owners were quick to seize upon and which was to lead to a substantial expansion of the railway network and coal traffic around Dunston.

Chapter Eleven

The Dunston Extension
and the Derwenthaugh Branch

To the south of Tanfield, around Annfield Plain, Stanley and Stella Gill (not to be confused with Stella on the Tyne west of Blaydon), lay a flourishing group of collieries, which sent their coal for export to staiths at Jarrow by the Pontop and Shields branch of the NER, once part of the Stanhope and Tyne Railway. East of Stella Gill the line had been upgraded for locomotive working in 1856 but from Carr House near Consett to Stella Gill, the route was largely a series of rope-worked inclines. Dissatisfied with the congestion on the line and the long haul to the lower Tyne, a group of mine owners headed by Sir George Elliot, promoted a Bill in Parliament in 1885 for a West Durham and Tyne Railway, running from Pelton via Birtley to new staiths to be built at Dunston. The scheme included running rights over NER tracks to Cold Rowley near Consett, Lamesley, Tyne Dock and into Newcastle Central. Much of the route lay close to the NER main line along the Team valley.

Despite being opposed by the NER on the grounds of the excellence of its existing shipping facilities at South Shields and the low freight rates charged, the Commons saw no reason why the coal owners should not have their own railway if they so wished and passed the Bill. However the Lords, in view of the duplication of routes and unnecessary expenditure of capital involved, wisely saw the matter differently and, upon the NER agreeing to provide the desired facilities, which was probably the aim of the coal owners all along, threw the Bill out. The NER then put forward the Dunston Extension Railway Bill which was given the Royal Assent on 23rd May, 1887.

The NER Bill included powers to build a six mile line between Annfield Plain and Stella Gill which, together with the Loud Bank Deviation line completed in 1886, by-passed the rope-worked inclines on the old Pontop and Tyne route (*see maps pages 90 & 92*). The line was steeply graded, much of it at 1 in 50 and 1 in 60 with a short length at 1 in 35. In later years this section achieved some fame among railway enthusiasts as the route of the heavily loaded iron ore trains from Tyne Dock to Consett.

Work on the Dunston Extension began in 1890, the first pile for the staiths at St Omer's Haugh just east of the mouth of the Team* being driven on the 26th August. At the southern end of the line, trains from Stella Gill and the Annfield deviation joined the East Coast Main Line (ECML) at Ouston Junction and travelled north to Low Fell Junction, from where the actual Dunston Extension line passed north-west across the Team valley before turning north into Norwood Coal Yard which served the staiths. Although the valley floor was both wide and level, virtually the entire line from Low Fell, including the over two acres of the coal yard, was raised on an embankment in order to maintain the necessary 35 ft clearance above high water at the staiths. The line, double track throughout, crossed Lobley Hill Road, the Team, the Team Waggonway,

* Although officially known as Dunston Staiths, being mainly on the eastern side of the Team they were actually in the then Borough of Gateshead.

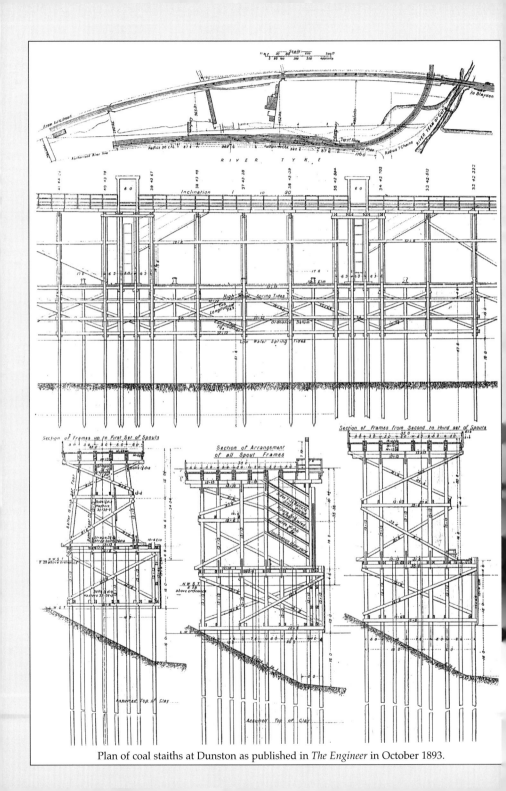

Plan of coal staiths at Dunston as published in *The Engineer* in October 1893.

the Tanfield branch and Ellison Road on plate-girder bridges on stone abutments. The limited clearance under the road bridges had the unlooked-for effect in later years of preventing the use of double-decked buses on many routes in the area.

From Norwood Junction south of the coal yard a double-tracked loop line passed along the west side of the yard, crossed Gasworks Road on a four-track, plate-girder bridge which also carried the staiths approach lines, turned westward down a steeply graded, nine chain curve, crossed the Team again and joined the Redheugh branch at Dunston East Junction. Here a small bridge-mounted signal cabin spanning the tracks controlled the junction and the adjacent level crossing. The loop line provided a useful route for goods traffic between the Carlisle line and the ECML to the south, bypassing the congestion at Newcastle Central and the High Level Bridge. It also gave traffic from the Tanfield branch and the Team Waggonway access to the Dunston Extension line and the new staiths, which although three reversals were involved, offered an alternative to the steep haul up the Redheugh incline.

The staiths, designed by the NER Northern Division Chief Engineer C.A. Harrison (who also designed the King Edward Bridge), were 1,709 ft in length and about 50 ft across at the widest point. Built of American pine the staiths were at the time probably the largest timber structure in Britain. After crossing the Redheugh branch a six chain curve led eastward out over the Tyne onto the main part of the staith, about 1,150 ft long, which lay roughly parallel to the river bank. The outer (north) side had three ship berths, each berth having two gravity loading spouts 87 ft apart, with clearance above high water of 35 ft for the landward set and 43 ft for the outer (eastern) set. Two rail tracks ran the full length along the outer side, with a third along about three-quarters of the length and a fourth at the widest part near the landward end. The staith deck was laid to a gradient of 1 in 96, falling towards the landward end, to allow empty waggons to be run off into the coal yard by gravity. The contractor was H.M. Nowell and the total cost was £210,000, a bargain as it turned out for all concerned.

The extension line and the staiths were officially opened on 16th October, 1893, the work having been delayed by bad weather and difficulties in obtaining sound foundations for the staiths, but the memorable ceremonies of the Carlisle line opening 54 years earlier were not repeated. The Annfield Plain deviation opened for goods traffic on the 13th of the following month and for passengers on 1st February, 1894, when to carry the increased traffic, the ECML was quadrupled by the addition of a pair of slow lines laid to the west of the existing tracks between Ouston and Low Fell Junctions.

The new staiths were a success from the start, shipping over 1½ million tons of coal in the first full year of operation. So successful in fact, that within a year or two, delays due to congestion were becoming so frequent that the NER decided to increase their capacity. The stretch of the Redheugh branch opposite the staiths was shifted 150 ft to the south, enabling a nine acre basin with an entrance 93 ft wide to be dredged out between the existing staiths and the river bank which was protected by a massive quay wall. Work was delayed for some time when the new quay wall collapsed in November 1905. The staiths were widened to accommodate two more rail tracks to service three ship berths

Dunston staiths in the early 1930s - typical for the period, the colliers are generally small in size (note the tiny vessel at the furthest outer berth) and almost all of the 'three island' type with engines amidships. More ships are moored in the river waiting for loading berths. A grain carrier is unloading at the flour mill in the left background. Part of the Redheugh branch and the gas works in the foreground. *Beamish Museum*

Dunston Station 1909-1926. A single island platform with a ramp leading down to it from the Ellison Road overbridge. The coal cells were a characteristic feature of NER stations. Hopper waggons were pushed up onto a track raised over the cells when the coal could be dumped straight into the storage area rather than the system usual elsewhere of laboriously unloading side-door wagons by hand. The scheduled passenger service was withdrawn in 1926 but the goods yard remained in use until 1965.

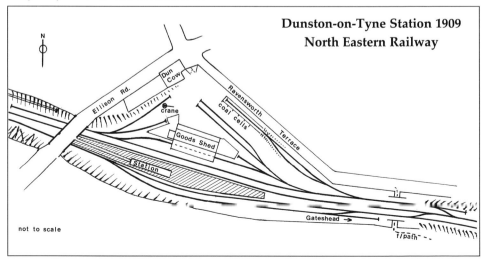

**Dunston-on-Tyne Station 1909
North Eastern Railway**

N

Dun Cow

Ellison Rd.

crane

Ravensworth Terrace

coal cells

Goods Shed

Station

Gateshead →

not to scale

T/path

facing the new basin, the 'new side' and equipped similarly to the outer berths which became the 'old side'. The Redheugh loop line junction, Dunston Staiths Junction (later Norwood Junction No. 2), was shifted 250 yards to the south-east, the existing two-track bridge across Ellison Road being now being used solely for the loop line. A new plate-girder bridge over Ellison Road carried five approach tracks into the greatly enlarged coal yard which, with 16 tracks, now covered over seven acres. A new through-girder bridge carried four more tracks across Gasworks Road onto the staiths. The new facilities came into use in 1909.

Meanwhile further extension of the rail network in the area had occurred with the construction of the Derwenthaugh branch (*see map page 90*). From a junction with the Redheugh branch at Derwenthaugh the line crossed the wetlands west of Dunston on an embankment, then through a deep cutting south of the village (as it then was) to join the Dunston Extension line at Norwood Junction (Norwood Junction No. 1). The south side of the cutting had a distinctive herring-bone array of stone-filled drainage channels, now largely obscured by scrub and undergrowth, while at the eastern end next to the Ellison Road bridge there was a fine collection of pigeon lofts, those ubiquitous features of the northern railway scene. Two large iron pipes ran along the top of the cutting on the north side; these carried gas from the Norwood coke ovens to fuel one of the boiler units at Dunston 'A' Power Station.

The Derwenthaugh branch was opened for mineral traffic on 29th August, 1904 and for goods on 1st April, 1905 when Dunston (284 years after its first railway) now received its first station. Situated on the new Derwenthaugh branch immediately to the east of the Ellison Road bridge, the station was for general goods and domestic coal traffic only. The facilities included a goods shed, sidings, loading docks with a crane and a set of coal cells. Coal cells were a characteristic feature of almost all NER stations. Domestic coal merchants elsewhere in Britain usually received their supplies in their own, small-capacity wagons which had to be laboriously unloaded by hand through side doors. In contrast, on the NER, domestic coal was generally delivered to the merchants in company-owned hopper waggons which were unloaded over a set of coal cells. These consisted of a row of open-fronted brick or stone cells or bunkers across which one or sometimes two, rail tracks were carried on heavy wooden beams or steel girders. Wagons were positioned over the required cell and the load dropped into the space underneath. The arrangement was very efficient as unloading could be completed in minutes allowing the wagon to be returned into revenue earning service with little or no delay. The method was perpetuated by the LNER and lasted into BR days until the demise of the small station and the disappearance of the trade.

The next line to be built was the Dunston to Gateshead Link which opened for goods traffic on 22nd April, 1907 (*see map page 90*). Leaving the Dunston Extension at Allerdene Junction (Norwood Junction No. 3) the link line went north-eastward on an embankment before tunnelling beneath the ECML, to join it at King Edward Bridge West Junction. The bridge had been opened on 1st October, 1906 to give access from the ECML into the west end of Newcastle Central and avoid the hitherto necessity of main line trains having to reverse at Newcastle. On 1st January, 1909 Dunston finally got its own passenger station giving a service between the village and Newcastle Central via the Gateshead Extension, Gateshead West station and the High Level Bridge.

A short link, the Atlas Curve, between Dunston West Junction on the Redheugh branch and Whickham Junction on the Derwenthaugh branch, was opened for goods traffic on 16th June, 1908. This allowed the length of the Redheugh line west of Dunston West Junction to be reduced to sidings serving the power station and some other industrial sites.

The Derwenthaugh branch bypassed the busy section of the Redheugh branch through Dunston with its many industrial sidings and the difficult curve across the Team, and via the Dunston Extension line, gave a direct link between the Carlisle line and the ECML. The Dunston-Gateshead link similarly provided a through route between the Carlisle line and the south Tyneside and Sunderland region, avoiding the congestion at Newcastle Central and enabling the expensive-to-operate Redheugh incline to be closed in about 1907. The upper end of the incline was abandoned and the cutting filled in, which gave some much needed space for the expansion of the NER Gateshead Works. The lower end of the incline retained a single rail track well into the 1950s, apparently being occasionally used as a headshunt for the gas works. The Redheugh quay and rail link remained in use for some years after World War II carrying scrap metal from a small shipbreaking yard cutting up redundant warships.

Although not directly connected with Dunston, the final extension of the network of rail routes in the area was the opening in 1923 of the Bensham Loop which formed a triangular junction across the Dunston and Gateshead Extension lines and effectively completed the quadrupling of the ECML between Newcastle Central and Ouston Junction (*see map page 90*).

Signals on the new lines were standard NER lower quadrant semaphores on steel lattice posts or gantries. At Norwood the coal yard approaches, the three Norwood Junctions and Dunston station were controlled from a large bridge-mounted signal cabin with 85 levers. Opened in 1903 it was a prominent landmark high on the embankment over the Redheugh loop line.

The early years of the 20th century saw the output of coal mined in Britain rise from 225 million tons in 1900 to 287 million tons in 1913, an increase of 28 per cent. In 1904 3.24 million tons were shipped from Dunston. Lured by the apparently unassailable prosperity of their coal business, the NER Directors, not unreasonably, decided upon further expansion of their coal shipping facilities at Dunston by erecting a second set of staiths about a mile upstream from the earlier set. The Atlas Curve had allowed the closure of that part of the Redheugh branch to the west of Dunston West Junction and much of site was now obliterated by the approach tracks and coal yard for the new West Dunston staiths. The truncated western end of the Redheugh branch remained to provide access to Dunston 'A' Power Station. The West staiths (contractor Mitchell Bros Ltd) were opened on 1st February, 1914. In marked contrast to the Team staiths, the new facility must have been a poor investment. Plagued by the trade depression of the 1920s and the General Strike of 1926 and the associated miners' strike which dragged on for some six months, the staiths proved uneconomic and were closed in 1930. The rail tracks were lifted but the staith structure remained until after World War II as a derelict reminder of what might have been.

Staith Operation

Dumping coal into ships might appear to be a fairly simple procedure. It wasn't. Unlike most rail traffic, coal trains for the staiths ran 'as required', with consequential varying demands on the availability of locomotives, waggons and train crews although many of the colliers, particularly those supplying the London industrial market, ran more or less regular trips. The coal trade itself was subject to fluctuations as demand varied with the time of year and, over longer periods, with economic conditions. To allow better control of their vessels ship masters and the river pilots preferred to steam up river against the ebbing tide which meant that several ships might arrive at Dunston in quick succession. Each ship would require a pre-arranged tonnage of a specific type - steam coal for boilers, gas coal, coking coal, domestic fuel, coke, ships' fuel, pencil-pitch.* All this had to be railed to the coal yard from the correct colliery at the appropriate time; a ship kept waiting and unproductive would not be popular with ship-owner or customer. Nevertheless at busy periods it was not unusual for ships to be kept moored at buoys in the river next to the staiths or at mooring posts (dolphins) in the basin waiting for berthing.

The actual loading required skill and foresight. With all six ship berths operating, each vessel needing a specific type and tonnage, a set of waggons sent to the wrong chute on the staith would result in delay and disruption of loading and undoubtedly some harsh words for the yard foreman and shunters from the staith superintendent.

The Staithes, Dunston-on-Tyne.

Another view of the staiths from the river. Business is good, ships are waiting for berths and one appears to be double parked! *Beamish Museum*

---

* Pencil pitch, in the form or short rods for ease of handling, was produced by the Thomas Ness tar works from 1971.

Work on the staiths was hard, dirty and, particularly before electric lighting was installed in 1930, dangerous. Accidents were not unusual particularly during night work and in cold and icy conditions. The dirtiest job and rightly also the best paid was that of the trimmers who worked in the holds of the colliers spreading the coal evenly into the sides and corners to maintain the vessel's trim. Teeming coal by gravity down the spouts always resulted in a good deal of breakage which reduced the value of the coal. In later years electric conveyers were installed and coal could be lowered right into the ship's hold; this and the wider hatch covers on the more modern ships, also reduced the amount of trimming needed to spread the load.

A single spout could load some 8,000 tons in a normal day, close to 50,000 tons daily for the whole staith at a busy time; the coal yard sidings could hold 5,000-6,000 tons in wagons. Obviously empties had to be removed and loaded trains brought in and sorted with great efficiency if the system was not to collapse in chaos. In addition it must be remembered that the Dunston Extension, Derwenthaugh and Redheugh branches were also handling the thousands of tons of coal needed by the power station, gas works, and coke ovens as well as the many smaller users in the area. It was easy to believe that the sole function of the railway was to serve the coal industry. All this activity was the onerous responsibility of the yard master and staith superintendent. The difficulty of fitting scheduled passenger trains into this traffic can be imagined and the apparent wish of the LNER in the 1920s to close the train service to Dunston station appreciated.

Dunston staiths in the 1980s, an aerial view looking south from above Scotswood. Not a ship to be seen, even the dolphins (mooring posts) and buoys have gone. The mouth of the Team is just to the right of the landward end of the staiths. The area south of the staiths, including the site of the coal yard and most of the gas works, is being cleared and developed for the 1990 National Garden Festival. *Beamish Museum*

Chapter Twelve

The Waggonways in the
19th and 20th Centuries

By 1923 the railway network around Dunston had reached its greatest extent, most of the development having taken place during the last 30 years, driven mainly by the demands of the coal trade (*see maps pages 90 & 92*). By this time the Tanfield branch and Team Waggonway had been carrying coal to Dunston for over two centuries. The routes of the Team Way and the remaining length of the Western Way were now conventional, locomotive-operated branch lines but the Tanfield branch, by virtue of its two gravity operated inclines, could still lay claim to the old title of waggonway.

The Team Waggonway

Lee (*see Bibliography*) described the Tanfield Way as the 'world's oldest railway' but this would better describe the Team Way which had been carrying coal to Dunston for 54 years before the first waggons trundled down the Tanfield line. Early in the 19th century the pits in the Team valley which used the Team Way were connected by a series of inclines climbing up the eastern side of the Team Valley to connect with the Ouston Waggonway, later known as the Pelaw Main railway. Coal could then be shipped either from Dunston or via the Pelaw route to staiths lower down the Tyne at Heworth. Steam locomotives replaced horse haulage in 1868.

Norwood Coking Plant, opened in 1912, straddled the Team line which supplied it with coal from the Pelaw Main collieries. From 1962* the plant was connected by a short spur line to the Dunston Extension line just east of Norwood Junction and the old link with the Tanfield branch at Teams Crossing was abandoned. The development from 1937 of the Team Valley Trading Estate to the south of Norwood resulted in some realignment of the line which now served some of the new Estate factories which were also given a connection with sidings leading off the ECML.

By the 1930s shipment of coal from the old Team staiths had long ceased and the northern remnant of the line on a low embankment along Clockmill Lane (then an ash-surfaced, generally muddy track) beyond the Team Crossing was near derelict. Earlier it had served a couple of small industrial sites but latterly it had seen only occasional use as a waggon stand. In 1963 the section from north of the Team Valley Trading Estate to the Norwood Coking Plant was closed, the plant still being served by the connection with the Dunston Extension. The world's oldest railway finally closed in 1963 after nearly three centuries of continuous service to the coal industry, from the Restoration years of Charles II almost to the end of steam traction in Britain.

---

* Warn (*see Bibliography*) gives 1962 but the connection is shown on the 1947 2½ in. Ordnance Survey map.

Team Crossing in 1920. The road from Dunston to the Teams crosses from left to right behind the signal box. The signals are typical NER wooden semaphores with the signal arm acting in a slot in the post. The track in the foreground and heading into the distance is the last remnant of Team Way along Clock Mill Lane. The curved track on the right is the loop line linking the Tanfield branch and the Team Way. The waggons in the right background are empties waiting to go over the crossing and up the incline. *D.G. Charlton*

The Tanfield Branch

Following the revitalisation of the Tanfield line by the Brandling company, it had become the major outlet for coal from the Marley Hill-Tanfield district. Marley Hill colliery alone, reopened by John Bowes in 1840, produced some 270,000 tons of coal and coke in 1867.

In 1881 locomotives replaced horses on the level stretches of the line and on the stationary engine-worked Causey Wood East and West inclines. The engine house at Bowes Bridge was converted into a shed to house the branch locomotives. A new shed was built in about 1942 when the old one burnt down. An unusual occurrence of coal being carried *up* the inclines was the Saturday-only working of two loaded waggons from Redheugh to Sunniside by adhesion only, by a pair of locomotives. This may have been locomotive coal for the Bowes Bridge engines. The Tanfield Moor incline was closed in 1947 and East Tanfield pit switched to road transport in 1958 before finally closing in 1965. With the closure of Tanfield Lea, the Bowes Bridge engine shed and the branch south of the foot of Fugar incline were abandoned on 10th September, 1962. When Watergate colliery closed in 1964, the Lobley Hill incline was no longer needed and from 18th May, 1964 the Tanfield branch was reduced to the short level section from the foot of the incline to Redheugh on which the track remained until 1984.

Incline Operation

The Tanfield inclines at Lobley Hill and Fugar Bank were gravity operated as self-acting, balanced inclines, an extremely efficient system where the loaded traffic was always downhill. The two sets of waggons, loaded and empty, were attached to the ends of a rope which passed over a large horizontal pulley at the top of the incline. When the loaded set was released it pulled the empty set up to the head of the incline; speed was controlled by a brake on the rope wheel. Horizontal rollers laid between the rails supported the rope and prevented it from dragging on the ballast. Vertical rollers were used where necessary to prevent the rope from fouling lineside structures at the top and bottom of the run and on curved stretches of track such as occurred on the Lobley Hill incline. The track layout on self-acting inclines was unusual. At the upper end three rails were laid, the middle rail being common to both tracks. At the half-way point, the 'meetings', the rails diverged into normal double track to allow the two sets of waggons to pass while below the meetings a single track was laid to the bank foot. The descending waggons automatically reset the points at the lower end of the meetings so that when empty, the set returned up the same side. At Lobley Hill however, the upper end of the incline was laid with normal double track; because of the curve in the track the usual three rail layout would have resulted in the rope attached to the ascending waggons lying across the path of the descending waggons and it was not possible to place the tall vertical guide rollers between the rails where they would have fouled the waggons. At the bottom of the incline the rope was slipped by the bank rider, the modern

The top of the Lobley Hill incline on the Tanfield branch. A loaded set of steel 21 ton hopper waggons is starting its descent with the rope attached to the ascending set on their left. The outermost raised tracks are the kips which prevent the empty returning wagons from running back down the incline when the rope is slipped. The site of the photograph can be identified today by the Roman Catholic Church in the left background.   *Beamish Museum*

Lobley Hill incline - the same set of waggons on its way to the foot of the incline – Arthur's Hill in Newcastle in the distance.   *Beamish Museum*

equivalent of the old-time waggoner, who rode on the last waggon of the set, holding on to a handrail and standing on the buffer casting, which on NER waggons, had a small footstep on the upper side for the purpose. After slipping the rope at the bottom of the Lobley Hill incline the waggons were allowed to run on over the Team crossing under the control of the shunter who ran alongside to operate the waggon brakes. Sometimes he would place his shunting pole under the waggon sole bar and over the brake handle and perch on the end to get extra braking power, a practice reminiscent of the old-time waggoner's habit of sitting on the convoy, and actually 'expressly forbidden' by the railway company rule book. The level crossing gates were closed before the waggons were released from the top of the incline resulting in tedious delays to road traffic for no obvious reason to the general public, before the waggons trundled slowly across the road. On the uphill run the bank rider might be seen nonchalantly perched on the buffer of the leading waggon, facing up the hill, leaning back against the waggon and lighting up his Woodbine. The empty set arriving at the top of the incline ran into a depression, the kip, which prevented it from retreating back down the hill when the rope was slipped by the bank rider at the critical point.

The Team Crossing was probably unique. Dating as a road crossing from the opening of the Team Way in 1670 and, after the opening of the Tanfield Way, being the crossing point of two of the world's oldest railways (in the middle of a main road!) it must have been the world's oldest level crossing.

So, after nearly 300 years of operation, the Tanfield and Team Waggonways, two of the world's oldest continuously-worked railways faded into history.

The Western Way

However part of the route of Jane Clavering's Third Western Way between Winlaton Mill and Derwenthaugh staiths, still survived as part of the Chopwell and Garesfield Railway (*see maps pages 90 & 92*). The staiths closed in 1960 and with the closure of Chopwell colliery the following year the line from the colliery to Winlaton Mill also went, but the stretch of the old way between Clockburn Drift and the Derwenthaugh locomotive shed at Swalwell remained in use. Clockburn Drift had been driven underground between Marley Hill colliery and Winlaton Mill in 1952 to carry coal by a double track 3 ft 6 in. gauge, diesel-hauled system to supply the Derwenthaugh Coking Plant. The coking ovens were rebuilt in 1971 but with the closure of the plant in 1986 the last of the area's waggonway routes ceased to exist. In view of the Grand Allies' concerted attempts to put her out of business, it was rather ironic that part of Jane Clavering's Western Way should outlive those of her rivals.

A train on the Tanfield branch near Andrew's House, now the site of the Tanfield Railway . station. The locomotive is LNER class 'N10' 0-6-2T No. 1716, built at Darlington as NER class 'U' in 1903. Based at Gateshead Shed it would have spent its working life in the Dunston area before being withdrawn from service in 1962. Note the great variation in wagon type - the fifth wagon is one of the distinctive NER 20 ton wooden hoppers. *Beamish Museum*

It is 1952 - little more than the derelict platform remains of the first Dunston passenger station, and there is not much happening in the adjacent goods station although this is still open for business. The characteristic NER coal cells can be seen in the left background in front of the houses in Ravensworth Terrace. Two of the sidings are occupied by loaded coal wagons intended for the staiths. Some of the old wooden hopper wagons are still in use. *J.W. Armstrong Trust*

Chapter Thirteen

Goods and Mineral Traffic in the 20th Century

Mineral traffic - coal, coke, iron ore and limestone - was the lifeblood of the NER and provided a substantial proportion of the company's revenue. However, while in the early years of its existence working expenses as a proportion of gross income were around 45 per cent, by the first decade of the 20th century expenses had risen to over 60 per cent of revenue. Dividends, which had peaked at 9 per cent in the early 1870s, fell to between 5 per cent and 7 per cent by the turn of the century and the company looked for ways of increasing the efficiency of its operations. One of the visible signs of this policy was the simplification of the livery used on mineral locomotives and rolling stock. A more significant change was the introduction of larger wagons* and more powerful locomotives and this was reflected in the receipts for mineral traffic which rose from 7s. 8d. per train mile in 1900 to 13s. 10d. in 1910, an increase of 80 per cent. Over the same period returns from passenger traffic were virtually static at about 3s. 9d. per train mile.

Wagons

On most railways in Britain until Nationalisation, coal was carried almost exclusively in wagons of 8 to 12 tons capacity, unloaded through side doors and owned not by the railway companies, but by the individual collieries and coal merchants. Such Private Owner wagons were not common in the North East except on the colliery-owned lines such as the Bowes Railway. In the first years of the new century the NER, as part of its efforts to improve the efficiency and profitability of its mineral business, began experimenting with larger wagons and from 1903 settled on what became the distinctive NER hopper wagon of 20 tons capacity. The high, wooden body sides sloped inwards towards the sole bars betraying its chaldron waggon ancestry. The ends were reinforced with two massive vertical wooden stanchions which were extended below the buffer beam to enable the wagons to buffer up to the chaldron waggons still common in the pit yards. In later years these extensions were omitted from new stock and sawn off the older wagons. Like the majority of British freight stock they were loose coupled and without continuous brakes.

The 20 ton hoppers were very successful; between 1900 and 1912 the average load of a mineral train almost doubled from about 184 tons to 365 tons. Twenty-four of the new wagons with a tare weight of 196 tons could carry 480 tons of coal; the same load would need 40 wagons of 12 ton capacity and 292 tons tare. In addition to the extra 96 tons tare weight, the locomotive would have had to overcome the rolling resistance of an extra 16 vehicles. In 1902/3 the company built some steel 32 and 40 ton bogie hopper wagons some of which were fitted with Westinghouse or vacuum brakes and automatic couplings. Unfortunately this forward-looking enterprise came to nothing, apparently because few colliery owners were able or prepared to adapt their loading gear to accommodate the larger vehicles.

* The modern spelling is adopted from here onwards, although not by NER until later.

71

The sidings at the bottom of the Lobley Hill incline in British Railways days. A class 'J72' (ex-class 'E1') is shunting empty wagons waiting to go up the incline. The modern steel upper-quadrant bracket signal contrasts with old NER wooden lower-quadrant type in the background. *I.H. Hodgson/J.W. Armstrong Trust*

NER 'T' class (LNER 'Q5') 0-8-0 No. 2122. Wilson Worsdell's 'T'/'T1' 0-8-0 is often regarded as one of the most handsome of British mineral engines, particularly as the first examples appeared in fully-lined green livery. From 1904 the livery for goods engines was black with fine red lining and, from 1928, plain (and usually dirty) black. Class 'T1' was identical except for having slide valves in place of piston valves. No. 2122 was built at Gateshead in 1901 and worked heavy coal trains until 1950. *Rail Archive Stephenson*

In 1923 the London & North Eastern Railway (LNER) inherited over 18,000 NER 20 ton mineral wagons and continued to build the same type with only minor changes such as the replacement of the wooden end stanchions by steel T-section. Some of the 20 ton hoppers were adapted to carry powdered coal for Dunston 'B' Power Station by fitting dust proof seals to the hopper doors and adding a steel frame over the top to take a weather-proof tarpaulin cover. From 1936 an all-steel version of the 20 ton wooden hopper was introduced and gradually replaced the old type, some of which nevertheless survived into the 1950s and even later on some National Coal Board lines. In 1905/6 the NER had experimented with a small batch of all-steel, 23 ton hoppers closely resembling the type eventually produced by the LNER. To improve productivity during World War II the 20 ton wagons were allowed to carry 21 tons.

NER mineral stock was painted grey with originally the company name in full in white letters shaded black; later only the initials NER were applied and the shading was omitted. The LNER used a lighter grey and white unshaded lettering as did BR, but latterly the colour scheme was best described as muck and rust. Brake vans, essential to control loose-coupled goods and mineral trains not fitted with continuous brakes, were painted brown with yellow lettering on both the NER and LNER.

Goods Traffic

Until the 1960s the railways carried a substantial traffic in 'smalls', items such as parcels and other merchandise insufficient to form a wagon or van load. Dunston goods station had its share of this business and the railway operated a road delivery and collection service in the area, provided originally by a horse-drawn rolley (a flat bed, four-wheeled wagon). From about the 1930s the 'hayburner' was supplanted by a motor van or the distinctive, railway mechanical horse, a petrol-powered, three-wheeled tractor unit (Karrier 'Cob'), with an articulated trailer. These were a common sight in the village, as was the (usually) hand-written sign in a shop window 'LNER please call' when a business had items for collection. Telephones were not all that common in the Dunston area in the 1930s.

Locomotives

Until the turn of the century the classic British 0-6-0 tender engine remained the standard for mineral haulage on the NER, reaching its final development in the 'P2' and 'P3' classes (LNER 'J26' and 'J27'), designed by Wilson Worsdell and built between 1904 and 1922. These engines have been described as little more than a large boiler on wheels, the combination of a 5 ft 6 in. diameter boiler on a short wheelbase giving them a powerful and massive appearance fully in keeping with their capacity for work. They frequently appeared at Dunston usually having worked coal trains from the Sunderland area. The drive for increased train loading in the early years of the 20th century naturally led to the introduction of a series of more powerful locomotives, the first of which, Wilson Worsdell's class 'T'/'T1'

An official photograph of 'E' class 0-6-0 (later LNER 'J71'). A very neat and attractive small shunting engine designed by T.W. Worsdell in 1886. No. 299 was scrapped after 'only' 50 years service - NER engines were remarkably long lived, many of this class lasted for more than 70 years. *Rail Archive Stephenson*

NER 'E1' (LNER 'J72') class 0-6-0. This was Wilson Worsdell's development of his brother's class 'E' with 4 ft 1 in. wheels in place of the 4 ft 7 in. of the 'E' class. No. 2173 is one of the later engines with Ross pop safety valves. The design was perpetuated by the LNER, and more remarkably, also British Railways, the last being built in 1951. *Rail Archive Stephenson*

(LNER 'Q5') 0-8-0s tender engines with outside cylinders appeared in 1901. Altogether 90 were built, the last in 1911. These engines with a large boiler which gave ample steam for the short but heavy haulage runs commonly needed in the colliery traffic, gave a significant increase in power of about 28 per cent compared to the earlier class 'P1' 0-6-0s which had come into service in 1898. During World War I 50 of the class were sent to France on loan to the Railway Operating Department of the Royal Engineers. After returning to the North East they were embellished with a brass replica of the RE badge and three service stripes, carried at first on the cab side and later on the front sandbox.

Vincent Raven, who followed Worsdell as Chief Mechanical Engineer (the new title) in 1910, developed the Worsdell's 0-8-0 design into class 'T2' (LNER 'Q6') of which 120 were built between 1913 and 1923, the last 50 coming from Armstrong-Whitworth's works at Elswick. While mechanically similar to the 'T'/'T1' and with only a small increase in tractive effort the 'T2' had a much larger boiler with a superheater. The 0-8-0 wheel arrangement with outside cylinders and a considerable front overhang was not a type suitable for speeds much over 30 mph but these engines were ideal for the slow, heavy haulage for which they were intended. With the full weight of the locomotive on the driving wheels, about 66 tons for a 'T2' they had ample adhesion and the steam brake, mechanically connected to the tender brakes, made the whole 110 tons available for braking, a valuable asset when handling a heavy train of unbraked coal wagons. The engine sheds at Borough Gardens (in Gateshead on the Sunderland line about one mile east of the High Level Bridge) and Blaydon maintained the fleets of 0-8-0s which dominated the coal traffic in North-West Durham. Shunting in the Norwood Yard and pushing wagons onto the staiths was done by class 'E' and 'E1' 0-6-0 tanks (LNER 'J71', 'J72'). Together with a pair of Sentinel four-wheeled, fully enclosed, geared engines (LNER 'Y3') known as 'pups' which shunted the wagons on the staiths, these were the only locomotives allowed on the staiths. The sight and sound of a 'J72' coupled behind eight or nine loaded hoppers charging down the coal yard at full regulator, exhaust erupting sky high and the wagons rocking round the curve onto the staiths with flanges squealing, is not easily forgotten. Sometimes the load was too much for the engine to reach the far end of the staith against the gradient and the wagons had to be taken back into the yard for another attempt. Empty wagons were allowed to run off the staith by gravity to accumulate behind a waiting 0-8-0.

While it was mainly concerned with passenger and main line goods locomotives, Gateshead Shed supplied the Norwood and local shunting engines and Bowes Bridge Shed, a subsidiary of Gateshead, normally had a pair of class 'U' (LNER 'N10') 0-6-2 tanks to handle traffic on the locomotive-worked stretches of the Tanfield branch. Towards the end of the steam era, ex-War Department 2-8-0s appeared on occasion and modern LNER types such as class 'K3' 2-6-0s replaced many of the old NER engines, to be supplanted in turn by the new diesels.

Express goods trains from the Forth goods station just to the west of Newcastle Central, were routed westward via the Carlisle line north of the Tyne and then over Scotswood rail bridge and back along the Derwenthaugh branch and Dunston Extension to join the ECML at Bensham Junction. These and through

The day's work done - two 'J72' class 0-6-0s and two Sentinel 0-4-0 geared engines ('pups') coupled together on the staiths approach line are waiting to return to Gateshead Shed.

J.W. Armstrong Trust

goods trains using the Derwenthaugh-Dunston Extension route provided a sight of more glamorous engines such as Gresley's 'V2' class 2-6-2s and Pacifics, and during the war years, a rare 'A4' class 4-6-2 streamliner or a genuinely exotic species in the shape of an LMS mixed traffic engine working through from Carlisle might be spotted. However railway activity around Dunston almost to the end of the steam era was best epitomised by a Raven 0-8-0 dragging a long train of loaded hopper wagons, or a 'J72' storming down the coal yard in full flight.

Originally all NER locomotives were turned out in fully lined, green livery but from 1904, as an economy measure (estimated to save £7,000 annually), goods and mineral engines were painted black with red lining. This was retained by the LNER until 1928 when unrelieved black became the standard for mineral engines, but as the years went by the engines, like the rolling stock, generally grew scruffier and deteriorated in appearance, although right to the end they never seemed to lose their capacity for hard work.

Chapter Fourteen

Industry at Dunston

The waggonways were owned, built and operated solely for the needs of the coal trade and profit of the coal owners. The new public railways, in contrast, were financed by the sale of shares to individual investors and were built to serve the general public, commerce and industry, offering transport on demand for both passengers and goods. One result of this was that the ready availability of rail transport, particularly for heavy goods and bulk commodities, enabled a great expansion of industry particularly in regions such as the North East where the canal system had never become established. The enormous growth of industrial activity, especially in the heavy engineering sector, which occurred during the Victorian era was dependent upon the railway for its establishment and very existence. While, especially in the Midlands and in Yorkshire and Lancashire, the canals usually continued to function, they were largely eliminated as serious competitors for the railway companies, often by the latter buying the canals and then neglecting or closing them altogether.

The effect on Dunston of the opening of the Newcastle and Carlisle Railway, the first public railway in the area, was considerable. The vital link of the Redheugh incline now allowed coal from the Pontop area and from the N&CR, which had until now been loaded into keels at Dunston and Redheugh, to be carried directly to the colliers down river. The keelmen obviously lost much of their work, no doubt to the satisfaction of the coal owners, the 'lads of coaly Tyne' being an independent lot given to striking. In 1840, 12 keel-berths of staith at Dunston were advertised for sale and on Bell's 1843 map of the coalfield the earlier branches of the Tanfield Way from the top of Lobley Hill to the Tyne at Dunston are no longer marked. However a contemporary illustration of the view westward from Gateshead, dated at about the mid-century, shows a steam tug towing four keels towards coal drops at Dunston, presumably the N&CR staiths handling coal from the Blaydon and Stella pits. It is not clear whether Ravensworth's Team staiths retained much of their traffic; Bell's map still shows the staith, but the loop line joining the Team Way to the Tanfield branch at Team Crossing gave the Ravensworth pits access to the down river route. However, although shipment of coal from the village in any quantity was not to resume for some 50 years, the effects of the new railways were not by any means negative.

Some industrial enterprises substantially predated the railway - Sir Ambrose Crowley's iron works at Low and High Team were begun in 1735; the works were later transferred to Swalwell where 'Crowley's crew' became famous for a wide range of iron products – 'Frey a needle tiv an anchor O'.†

There was a fulling mill* near the Team staiths in 1746 and the early years of the 19th century saw the establishment on the Tyne bank of Palmer-Hall's saw mill and the boatyards of Hedworth building racing skiffs, and Sadler building keels for the coal trade, yachts and wherries.

---

* Fulling was the treatment of cloth with heat and moisture to thicken and shrink it.
† 'From a needle to an anchor O'.

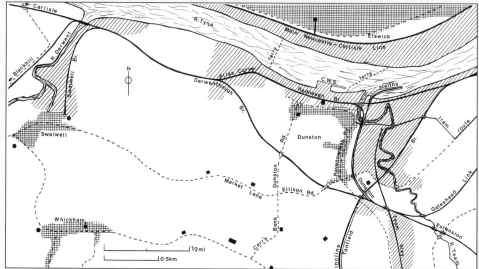

Industry and the railway *c.* 1900. Industry at this time is almost entirely dependent upon the railway for its transport needs, completely so in regard to the supply of coal. Only part of the Derwenthaugh branch and the Gateshead Extension are without some industrial activity. The unoccupied area between the Derwenthaugh branch and the south bank of the Tyne west of Dunston will later become the site of the NER West Dunston staiths and Dunston 'B' Power Station. The working class residential areas, other than the ancient village of Whickham, cling closely to the industrial zones on both sides of the Tyne. Despite being a heavily industrialised region the greater part of the area, as in most of Durham County, is farmland.

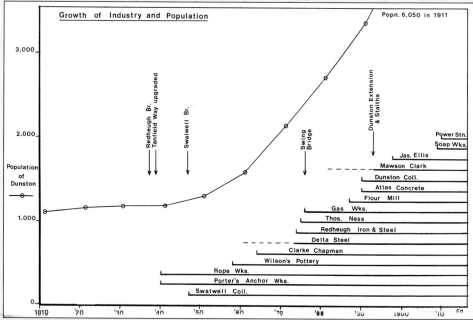

Growth of Industry and Population. The population of Dunston shows little change until the opening of the Redheugh branch of the Newcastle & Carlisle Railway in 1837. The subsequent steady growth of industry, dependent upon coal and the railway is mirrored by the increase in the population of the village.

The N&CR, while dependent on coal for part of its revenue, was a general carrier and the level stretch of open country along the Tyne bank at Dunston with a railway able to transport coal, raw materials and finished products running along its length, was a prime area for the establishment of heavy industry, as was the northern end of the Tanfield branch from the foot of the Lobley Hill incline to the junction with the Redheugh branch. From 1840 onward a steady growth of new industrial enterprises occurred along both lines.

While coal had long been the lifeblood of Dunston, the difficulty of draining the deeper coal seams had prevented mining on the low lying haughs and it was not until about 1840, after the arrival of the railway, that Norwood colliery just to the north of the Teams Crossing on the Tanfield branch was won, to be later bought by Bowes in 1849. Swalwell Garesfield colliery at the end of the Swalwell branch probably dated from the opening of the line in 1847. Dunston colliery was reopened by John Bowes & Co. in 1890, it having been worked briefly in about 1873. It was sold to the Swalwell Garesfield Coal Co. in 1899. The colliery was served by the Redheugh branch which had the greatest concentration of industry. At the Redheugh end, Carrick & Wardle's Foundry, started in 1873, lasted until about 1930 when it failed due to the depression in the chemical industry, its main customer. After World War II two small ship-breaking firms cutting up unwanted warships were established on the site. Westward of the Tanfield/Redheugh Junction, the great Redheugh Gas Works of the Newcastle & Gateshead Gas Company occupied the Tyne bank as far as the Team mouth, replacing an earlier group of small metal works and a tar works. A map dated 1884 shows the Dunston Brick Works and Thubron's saw mill near the Team mouth but these had gone by the 1940s. Later at the Team mouth were the engineering works of Taylor, Pallister & Co. Ltd and Emerson Walker Ltd. The Co-operative Wholesale Society (CWS) built its Dunston Flour Mill in 1887/91; an early example of reinforced concrete construction, the mill had its own jetty and imported grain by ship, much of it from East Anglia. In 1909 the CWS opened its Soap Works next to the flour mill. Next along the Tyne bank were Palmer Hall's long established saw mill and timber yard on either side of the Dunston Engine Works which made a great variety of heavy machinery particularly for the chemical, mining and quarrying industries.

On the landward side of the branch through the old village were Dunston colliery, Thomas Wardman's Glass Works, a iron and brass foundry and the well known Atlas Rivet works of McFarlane and Whitfield founded in 1889. Mawson Clark's Grease and Candle Works (c. 1905), were easily located by smell when the west wind blew across the village!

The modern age of electricity was heralded by the opening of the first Dunston Power Station (Dunston 'A') in 1910. This was replaced by the much larger Dunston 'B' Station, opened in 1933 but not completed to its full 320 megawatt capacity until after World War II. Originally designed to have six 50 megawatt generators, the two units added after the war were increased to 60 megawatts each. The boiler houses for the new units were taller than the earlier ones and rather spoiled the symmetry of what was an impressive early and successful example of steel frame and glass curtain wall construction. With its

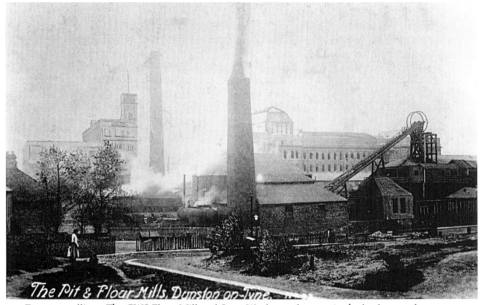

Dunston colliery. The CWS Flour Mill and Soap Works can be seen in the background.
Beamish Museum

The basin inside the flour mill jetty with the mill in the background on the right and the soap works to the left. The steam ferry is moored at its floating landing stage. It is low tide, the sailing vessel appears to be aground. A couple of timber-carrying keels are alongside Thubron's timber yard quay. *Beamish Museum*

The CWS Flour Mill - an early impression taken from the 'Co-operative & Wholesale Societies Ltd Annual' of 1910. In later years sail would disappear and modern suction gear would be installed for unloading the grain. *Beamish Museum*

The CWS Soap Works. This impression shows the works being well served, on the river side by sea-going vessels and lighters and on the land side by rail (the Redheugh branch) and horse-drawn road wagons. The steep curve across the Team in the line connecting the Redheugh branch with Norwood Junction is just visible curving away to the right in the left background. *Beamish Museum*

six, tall, free-standing chimneys it dominated the Tyne valley between Redheugh and Derwenthaugh. The older station survived throughout the war years as a standby emergency unit; the site was later occupied by the shipbreaking yards of Maple & Gillott and Clayton & Davies.

The West Dunston staiths and its sidings occupied the river bank to the west of the power station as far as the Delta Iron and Steel works of B.W. & G. Raine (c. 1874) and Cowen's coke ovens just to the east of the Derwent mouth. On the west side of the Derwent was the small set of staiths handling mainly coke carried by rail along the surviving fragment of the Third Western Way from the Winlaton Mill coke ovens of the Consett Iron Company.

On the Tanfield branch the two rope works of R.S. Newall and Dixon Corbitt were established in 1840. They were amalgamated in 1887, acquired by Hood Haggie & Co. in 1946 and eventually, in 1959, became part of British Ropes, and one of the longest surviving industries in the area. The rope works and the CWS flour mill and soap works were among the few industrial enterprises in the area which gave a significant level of employment to women.

The Tanfield line also serviced Emmerson Walker and Thompson's Dunston Forge at the foot of the Lobley Hill Incline, Davison's Glass Works (1868), the Redheugh Iron and Steel Co. (1874), and no fewer than three brick works and a 'manure siding'. An early enterprise on the Team Waggonway was a fertiliser works started by Thomas Ness in about 1875. This later developed into the Thomas Ness Tar Works which made a wide range of coal by-products derived from feed-stock from the neighbouring coke ovens. From 1955, block electrode pitch was produced for aluminium smelting at the Alcan works at Lynemouth and also exported via the staiths to Norway. The more easily handled 'pencil pitch' was made from 1971.

The adjacent Norwood Coke Ovens were opened in 1912 by Teams By-Product & Coke Co. Ltd and were supplied with coal from pits served by the Team Waggonway; it was taken over by Priestman Collieries in 1930 and eventually by the National Coal Board in 1947. In 1962 the old link with the Tanfield branch at Teams Crossing was abandoned and a connection remained with the Dunston Extension line near Norwood Junction.

On the Swalwell branch the Hannington foundry and engineering works were established in the late 1800s; later the works were taken over by Jas. Ellis and then Huwood Ltd. Hannington's also owned one of three brick works on the branch. Brick making seems to have been a speciality in the area during Victorian times. The site of the old Swalwell colliery was used by the National Coal Board as an open-cast coal disposal point from 1945 until the late 1980s.

Common to almost all these enterprises was their need for coal, notably the many thousands of tons consumed each week by the power station, gas works and the coke ovens, in addition of course, to the coal going to the staiths, all delivered by rail.

Industrial Railways

It is not easy at the present time to visualise the extent to which industry and commerce in the 19th and first half of the 20th century were dependent upon rail transport. Ordnance Survey maps of the Dunston area over this period show that virtually every industrial site, large and small, was connected to the railway. Indeed the larger concerns, the staiths, gas works, coke ovens and power stations were entirely dependent upon rail transport for their huge requirements of coal, amounts which at that time and place, would have been difficult or impossible to supply by any other means. Smaller concerns could be just as dependent upon the railway for their fuel supply and transport of raw materials and finished products. Even the Gateshead Union Workhouse at Low Fell had its own siding connected to the Dunston Extension line, probably for its coal supply. The only substantial industrial site in the area which I have been able to identify as not at any time having a rail link was the Team paper mill.

These private sidings typically ranged from a single track such as that serving Palmer's saw mill and shunted as required by the railway company, to the extensive internal systems of the gas works and power stations with their own locomotives. As an example of the extent of these industrial railways, the NER map of the 1,000 yards of the Redheugh branch between the Team bridge and Dunston West Junction shows no less than 12 sites with sidings connected to the railway. Dunston 'A' Power Station possessed over a mile of private sidings and both the gas works and the coke ovens had similarly large internal rail networks.

The larger private industrial rail systems throughout Britain were served by an army of small locomotives, virtually unknown to the general public and, until relatively recent times, often little regarded even by railway enthusiasts. Around Dunston, James Ellis Engineering (from 1903 to 1968), Delta Iron & Steel (from mid-Victorian times), both power stations, Mawson Clark's, the gas works and coke ovens all operated one or more industrial locomotives. The colliery-owned railways such as the Bowes Railway, and later the National Coal Board, maintained quite considerable fleets of locomotives; these varied from modern purpose-built industrial types to some remarkably ancient machines often bought second-hand from the large railway companies and given a new lease in life. Industrial engines came in a variety of forms; generally powerful for their size and with a short wheelbase suitable for the tight curvature of most works' tracks the classical type was a rather portly, 0-4-0 or 0-6-0 saddle tank engine with outside cylinders.

While this was the most common type, the power stations appropriately operated a number of electric locomotives, both battery powered and using overhead current supply, as well as in later years, diesel electrics and a Sentinel geared steam locomotive. The ubiquitous saddle tank, owned by the various contractors, also worked on the construction of the Dunston Extension, the Derwenthaugh branch and the two sets of staiths. Two 0-6-0 saddle tanks owned by H.M. Nowell, the contractor for Dunston staiths, were appropriately named *Dunston* and *Redheugh*.

Dunston 'B' Power Station in the late 1940s. The two new generator units and boiler houses at the east end (on the right) have been completed but the old 'A' Station further to the right has yet to be demolished. A dredger is working in the river.   *Beamish Museum*

Effects of Industry and the Railway on Dunston

By the end of the 19th century an almost continuous belt of industrial activity stretched along the Tyne bank from Redheugh to Derwenthaugh, along the Swalwell branch and along the Tanfield branch north of the foot of the Lobley Hill incline (*see graph page 78*). This was Industrial Britain at its peak. The steady growth of industry was matched by a parallel rise in Dunston's population attracted by the increasing availability of work. In the 50 years from 1841, the population rose from 1,192 to reach 3,325 in 1891, a rate of increase averaging 24 per cent over each 10 year period, about 70 per cent faster than that of the country as a whole.

The earliest maps show Dunston as a scatter of dwellings on the Tyne bank west of the Team. By the end of the Victorian period the village had grown in a narrow belt immediately to the south of the Redheugh branch and westward as far as the foot of Dunston Road and was spreading up Ravensworth Road. Later development was mainly from the Dun Cow Inn westward along Ellison Road and Market Lane, and it was not until the 1930s that houses appeared in the open area between the main roads and the park and on the farmland to the south of Ellison Road. The location of the early village, literally just across the road from the riverside industrial belt, would be a considerable advantage for working people who needed to live within walking distance of their employment before cheap, or indeed any, public transport became available. Some men did work at Armstrong's factories at Elswick which were easily reached by the steam ferry which operated from a floating stage near the flour mill or by Brymer's ferry from near the Dunston Engine Works, a rowboat and still in business in the 1930s.

While the railway brought great economic changes to Dunston, during the first half of the 20th century it also had an effect upon the social climate of the village. The Derwenthaugh branch could be crossed by the two road bridges and a footpath but of these, only the Ellison Road bridge carried any substantial traffic. The effect was to divide the newer residential development, mainly of semi-detached houses, south of the railway from the older terraces to the north which became, to some people, 'the wrong side of the tracks'. However, while both parts had schools and churches, the old village had most of the shops, the park, both cinemas* - and all the pubs!

In marked contrast to the industrial activity and growth in Dunston and Swalwell, the old village of Whickham, barely 1½ miles from the Tyne, remained throughout Victorian times and later, a quiet haven of mainly Georgian and Victorian houses. The fields to the south, once pockmarked with bell pits were now farmed (as much of it still is) and the only reminder of the once hectic days of the Grand Lease were the headworks of Whickhambanks colliery near the top of Swalwell Bank. Since the colliery had no rail link and was (presumably) solely a man-riding and ventilation shaft for either Swalwell or Axwell Park colliery it can have had little effect upon the village in an industrial sense.

Dunston, Swalwell and Whickham have all grown markedly particularly throughout the later part of the 20th century but, with the ready availability of public transport, increasing ownership of private cars and the replacement of heavy industry by service organisations, growth has been largely a result of development as dormitory suburbs of Gateshead and Newcastle rather than the earlier stimulus of industrial growth.

---

* Officially The Albert Picture Palace and The Imperial Hall, but old Dunstonians will remember them as the 'Top Hall' and the 'Bottom Hall'.

The first Dunston passenger station viewed from Ellison Road. Numerous goods wagons in the sidings and Norwood signal box can be seen in the background.   *Beamish Museum*

The recently completed King Edward Bridge (note the clean stonework) and the Redheugh incline in its last days. Three locomotives, a pair of tank engines and a 0-6-0 tender locomotive, the latter apparently one of Edward Fletcher's class '398' built in the 1880s, are 'shoving up'.

J.W. Armstrong Trust

Chapter Fifteen

Passenger Traffic

Dunston finally received a passenger station on 1st January, 1909 (*see maps pages 60 & 94*). The station, immediately to the east of the Ellison Road bridge, had a single island platform with access for passengers by a ramp down from the bridge. The station building was of timber construction with a canopy extending part way over the platform. The building provided the usual amenities and typically for the period had a selection of coloured enamel advertisements on its walls and a couple of slot machines. The timetable offered a service of 10 trains a day, on weekdays, in each direction between the village and Newcastle Central, via the High Level Bridge with an intermediate stop at Gateshead West. There was no service westward towards Blaydon.

The service was operated by an auto-train, a tank locomotive semi-permanently coupled between a pair of non-corridor compartment coaches. Each coach had a separate compartment with two 'porthole' windows at the outer end of the train for the driver who could operate the essential controls on the engine by mechanical linkages. The fireman remained on the footplate but could communicate with his mate by means of a speaking tube. The advantage of the auto-train on short branch services was that it avoided the necessity of uncoupling and running the engine around to the other end of the train for the return journey.

Auto trains were usually powered by 0-4-4 back* tanks of NER class 'BTP' (LNER 'G6') built between 1876 and 1884 to a design by Edward Fletcher. Originally typically Victorian in appearance, they had been modernised with new boilers and fittings by the time they appeared at Dunston. Locomotives were painted in the passenger livery of Saxony green lined in black with narrow white edging; while they carried the standard NER oval brass number plate they were unusual in that they did not display the company name or initials. The clerestory-roofed coaches were of panelled wood construction, finished in crimson lake with the company name and door labels such as 'First' and 'Guard' lettered in gold in a bold serif style elaborately shaded in pink, red, brown and black.

In 1911 the station issued over 44,000 tickets and by 1914 yearly passenger numbers had risen to a peak of over 73,000, despite which the cost of running the service exceeded the receipts. The station closed as a wartime economy measure on 1st May, 1918 but was reopened on the 1st October the following year. Competition from buses after the war led to the service being reduced to five trains a day with an extra evening train on Wednesday and Saturday, the route now being via the King Edward Bridge which eliminated the Gateshead stop.

The regular passenger service was finally withdrawn on 4th May, 1926 (at the start of the General Strike) but the station remained in use for occasional excursion traffic, particularly the popular Sunday School trips. Apparently in

---

* A tank locomotive in which the water was carried in a tank beneath the coal bunker rather than in the more usual side tanks.

the last years of the regular service, trains were often delayed at signals on King Edward Bridge, not a pleasant spot in winter; it was rumoured in the village that this was a deliberate move by the LNER to discourage passengers and enable the service to be withdrawn. In addition of course, the abandonment of the Gateshead stop was hardly a move to encourage use of the service. Whatever the truth, the removal of the passenger service enabled the line through Dunston to be operated by the permissive block system of signalling. This greatly facilitated the movement of mineral trains at busy periods in that it allowed more than one train to occupy a block section of track at the same time. It was not uncommon when coal traffic was heavy, to see two, sometimes three, coal trains standing head to tail through the station and the Dunston cutting waiting to clear the Norwood Junctions, a situation impossible under the absolute block system obligatory for passenger traffic.

Probably the last trains to use the station were specials evacuating children to villages in mid-Durham during the first days of World War II in September 1939. At some time during the war years the station buildings were demolished and the access ramp cut through to discourage vandalism but the platform remained, forlorn and overgrown with weeds. The goods station, however, remained in use until 5th July, 1965.

The apparently endless stream of coal trains passing through Dunston was occasionally varied by empty passenger-stock trains, usually hauled by 4-6-2 tank engines of ex-NER class 'D' (LNER 'A8') or the more modern LNER class ('V1'/'V3s', between Newcastle Central (which had little in the way of siding accommodation) and the coach storage sidings at Blaydon. Engineering work on the ECML, usually on Sundays, sometimes resulted in all main line trains being diverted through Dunston and Scotswood adding a touch of colour to the line.

Dunston's Other Railway

Early in the 20th century Dunston acquired a railway of a different kind. The Edwardian years saw the flowering on the streets of the larger towns and cities in Britain of the electric tramway, a public transport system whose virtues, long rejected particularly in Britain, are again becoming appreciated. As part of the modernisation and electrification of its originally steam-powered system the Gateshead and District Tramway Company was empowered by a Light Railway Order of 1900 to construct an extension of its Askew Road tram route, to Dunston via Pine Street (*see map page 78*). The line opened to the terminus at the Cross Keys near the foot of Ravensworth Road in July 1903. A proposed continuation up Ravensworth Road to the Dun Cow was abandoned. There was prolonged agitation for the line to be extended to Whickham but since the route up Dunston (Carr's) Bank involved gradients of the order of 1 in 9, this proposal, perhaps fortunately, came to nothing.

The single-deck bogie cars offered a frequent service, running every six or seven minutes in the morning and evening and every five minutes in the afternoon. The route was via Gasworks Road, Pine Street, Askew Road, the High Level Bridge and Westgate Road to the terminus outside Newcastle Central station. The service, while frequent, was rather slow, with a general speed limit of 12 mph and a maximum of 16 mph along part of Askew Road. The fare to Newcastle was 3*d*. which included payment to Newcastle Corporation for the use of their tracks in the city, in effect a revival of the old wayleave system. The front-exit cars, handsomely painted in crimson and white, were fitted with surprisingly comfortable, longitudinal wooden seats for about 44 passengers, with standing room for considerably more than were seated.

By 1950 trams were regarded in Britain as being out-of-date and obstructive of other road traffic and were being replaced almost everywhere by motor or trolley buses. Gateshead's trams, having been built in the 1920s, could reasonably be described by this time as verging on the antique. However their moment of glory came during the very severe winter of 1947 when for several days they were effectively the only public road transport operating on the snow- and ice-bound roads.

Packed solid with passengers, with more on the platforms and even standing on the outside bumpers (the conductors effectively gave up trying to collect fares), they faithfully trundled on through snow, ice and blizzard.

For the passenger perhaps the most memorable feature of the Dunston trams was the incredibly hard suspension - these trams must have had the hardest springs ever fitted to a road vehicle. Visitors to the Beamish Open Air Museum can sample the ride in one of these trams which has been preserved in full working order. In the final years of the service the company obtained some ex-Newcastle Hurst, Nelson Pullman cars - with padded seats and well-sprung bogies, these brought an unusual air of luxury to the Dunston line.

The end came on 4th August, 1951 when the Dunston service, the last privately-owned tram service in Britain, was withdrawn. The replacement double-deck buses were unable to pass under the staiths bridges and had to use an inconvenient and rather depressing and derelict turn-round point near the site of the old Ravensworth staith on Clock Mill Lane.

Dunston's other railway - a Gateshead and District Tramways tram preserved in full working order at Beamish. This car is one of a class of 20 built during the 1920s. Four of this type, but fitted with a different type of truck (bogie) with the large driving wheels at the outer ends, were allotted to the Dunston service. *Author*

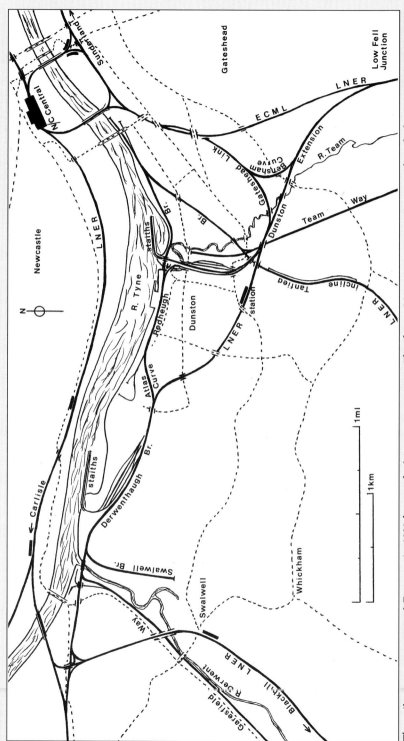

The railway system around Dunston in 1930 has reached its greatest extent. The three old waggonways still exist although the Team Way is almost moribund by now, and the West Dunston staiths will close this year. The complex network of interconnecting routes built by the NER and now part of the LNER occupy all three river valleys.

Chapter Sixteen

The LNER and Nationalisation

In 1923 the public railways of Britain were grouped into four major companies, the NER becoming part of the East Coast group, the London & North Eastern Railway. The numerous colliery-owned lines such as the Team Way and the Pontop and Jarrow (the Bowes Railway from 1932), however, remained with their current owners until eventually becoming the property of the National Coal Board in 1947.

Grouping had little visible effect upon the railways around Dunston. The familiar ex-NER locomotives continued to haul the trains, only the lettering changed and in 1946 they were given new numbers but the unrelieved black livery remained. The distinctive NER wooden hopper wagons were perpetuated by the LNER, to be gradually replaced from the mid-1930s by steel hoppers, a change that would almost certainly have taken place in any event. The network of company lines remained unchanged, but some development of private sidings occurred, for example for the new Dunston 'B' Power Station and on the new Team Valley Trading Estate which straddled and was served by the old Team Waggonway route. Following the erection in 1934 of a new road bridge over the Team Gut at St Omer's Haugh, a new channel was cut for the Team and the reclaimed land opposite the staiths was utilised for extra sidings for coke storage. Even as late as the 1950s the railways around Dunston retained essentially their pre-Grouping character and atmosphere; the noise and dirt of the staiths, ship sirens, the steam whistles and exhaust of the engines throughout the day and often into the night and the endless stream of coal trains. One of the few visible changes was the substitution of upper quadrant for lower quadrant arms on some of the more frequently used signals, although some of the earlier-style NER wooden, slotted-post signals still functioned on the older parts of the system such as the Tanfield branch.

On nationalisation, British Railways (BR) added 60,000 to the LNER engine numbers and tenders sported the new lettering or the BR lion and wheel totem but there was little other visible change. Only in the 1960s, towards the end of the steam era, did more modern ex-LNER locomotives appear on the coal traffic, to be replaced in turn by diesels.

Changes in Industry

Following a few years of euphoria immediately after the end of World War I Tyneside, almost entirely dependent upon heavy industry for such prosperity as it achieved, became a depressed and depressing area – the 1920s were the years of unemployment, the General Strike, the dole and the Jarrow Marches. One bright point was the opening of Watergate colliery on the Tanfield branch in 1926. However the following decade saw some revival of industrial activity which increased as the threat of war became more apparent. For Dunston and the railway's coal business the most significant event was the construction of the new Dunston 'B'

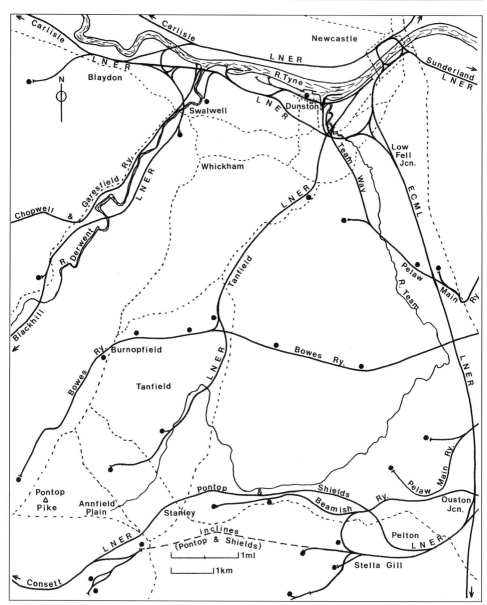

The coalfield *c.* 1932 is covered by a network of railways. The East Coast Main Line (ECML), the Carlisle, Blackhill, and Pontop and Shields lines carry passenger, goods and mineral traffic, the remainder including the privately owned colliery lines are generally restricted to coal traffic. By 1990 all the collieries will have gone and, apart from short preserved sections of the Tanfield branch and the Bowes Railway only the ECML, the line to Sunderland and the Carlisle route through Dunston will remain.

The Norwood Junctions looking eastward from the signal box windows in 1966. The locomotive, 'Q6' 0-8-0 No. 63395 (ex-NER 'T2' No. 2238) now preserved on the North Yorkshire Moors Railway, is heading for the staiths to pick up coal empties. The photograph was taken in February and the engine is fitted with a snowplough for working in the bleak Consett region. The low level tracks on the left are part of the Team Way. *A.R. Thompson*

Also seen from the Norwood signal box, a 'J27' Class 0-6-0 heads for Gateshead after leaving a load of coal at Dunston Power Station. A diesel multiple unit from Newcastle to Hexham is passing onto the Derwenthaugh branch. The coke ovens and tar works are in the background on the right. *A.R. Thompson*

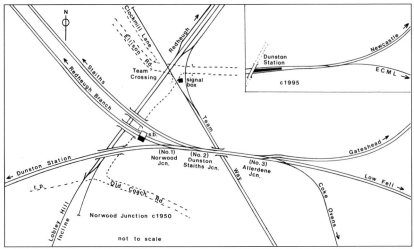

The Norwood Junctions and Team Crossing *c*. 1950. There is still fairly heavy coal traffic to the staiths but only diverted passenger trains pass through Dunston. The Tanfield branch is active but the Team Way beyond the unique Team crossing is moribund. By 1990 the coal traffic and almost all the tracks have gone but Dunston has had its passenger service restored with a new, if very basic, station.

Power Station by the North Eastern Electric Supply Company to replace the old 1910 station. Although not completed to its full size until the late 1940s the power station naturally led to a very significant increase in the amount of coal traffic on the railway. The 1930s also saw the establishment of the Team Valley Trading Estate but, while the site was connected to the railway system, the Estate was largely occupied by light industrial concerns with relatively little demand for coal. The only major coal-using industrial development in the years just after the end of World War II (other than the completion of the power station) occurred at the Norwood Coke Plant where two new ranges of coking ovens were built. At about this time some new workshops were constructed by the Redheugh Iron and Steel Company.

In the last days of steam in 1966, a 'J27' class 0-6-0 (ex-NER class 'P4') with empty steel hoppers from Dunston staiths pulls away from Norwood towards King Edward Bridge Junction via the Gateshead Link line. The driver appears to be giving the engine more steam to tackle the climb up to the main line. Sixty years old and still doing a hard day's work, the engine will be scrapped in 1967. The Dunston Extension line from Low Fell is on the left. *A.R. Thompson*

Chapter Seventeen

The End of the Coal Trade
and the End of the Railway

Coal is a finite resource and by the mid-20th century the North-West Durham coalfield had been mined for at least 700 years. As the early primitive mining techniques were slowly replaced by more efficient methods and the demand for coal grew ever greater, the rate of extraction had increased until, by the mid-20th century, the inevitable day when the workable deposits would be exhausted was in sight. When the coal ran out it seemed certain that the local rail network, almost entirely dependent upon the coal traffic for its existence, would be drastically reduced, if not closed completely.

Of the pits around Dunston, Swalwell-Garesfield and Norwood were closed as early as 1940, and Dunston colliery ceased work in 1947, although the pithead buildings remained until the 1980s.

When the coal industry was nationalised in 1947, the North-West Durham Area took over some 35 pits. Half of these had been closed by 1963 and the last, Kibblesworth, went in 1974. The close-knit mining communities had always lived with the threat of their local pit closing, perhaps to open again, perhaps not. Norwood colliery for example, opened by Bowes in 1849, was closed in 1875 but reopened with new owners in 1899. Now, however, the pit closures were permanent, there was no more coal to be won -

'Now me hewin' days are through, through,
Now me hewin' days are through

Throughout the 1960s and 1970s the demand for coal decreased as North Sea natural gas became widely available as an industrial and domestic fuel and the railways themselves turned to diesel power. While the bulk of the nation's electricity was still generated in coal burning stations, these were now being sited on or near the recently exploited coal deposits such as the great Selby coalfield. Mining in Durham County was now mainly restricted to some open-cast sites such as that at Pelton which obliterated part of the old Stanhope and Tyne route and to those collieries near the coast which could mine the substantial coal deposits under the North Sea.

The level of pre-war trade at Dunston staiths (just under 4 million tons in 1939) had never been regained - by 1973 annual shipments had fallen below 400,000 tons and single shift working was introduced. By this time the colliers serving the staiths were the only large vessels using the Tyne above the swing bridge and, when British Rail and the National Coal Board refused to pay the Tyne Commissioners for the dredging necessary to maintain navigation, the staiths ceased work in 1977 and were finally closed in 1980. Following the closure an upsurge in demand for coal for export led to an attempt by the Coal Board to re-open the facilities but it was too late - the men and their skill and knowledge had gone, retired or found other work.

The Redheugh Gas Works, made redundant by the availability of natural gas, were closed in 1967, the plant and buildings demolished and the site cleaned

The Newcomen engine at Tantobie being dismantled. This engine pumped water from a 200 ft shaft at Tanfield Moor colliery for over 120 years. *Beamish Museum*

The Margaret pit of Tanfield Lea colliery, served by the Tanfield branch and closed in 1960. *Beamish Museum*

The 1907 Gateshead link line descends to pass through the tunnel under the main line south, 27th February, 1977. *John Mallon*

Redheugh Gas Works Jn in 1969. The Tanfield branch comes in from the left to join the Redheugh branch at this point. *John Mallon*

The eastern end of the old side staiths and the entrance to the new basin, 8th April, 1977.
John Mallon

View to the west at the landward end of Dunston staiths on 10th April, 1977 with one of the loading spouts in the right foreground. The Co-operative Wholesale Society's mill in the distance had a siding connection with the Redheugh branch at Dunston East Jn.   *John Mallon*

up. Of the other major coal users, Norwood Coking Plant ceased work in the mid-1980s and the associated Tar Works followed in 1987. Dunston 'B' Power Station, after spending its last years as a standby facility, was closed in 1986 and this decade also saw the disappearance of much of the heavy industry such as the Redheugh Iron & Steel Company which had grown up along the railway lines. Within about a decade the continuous belt of coal-using industrial concerns which had grown over the previous one and a half centuries in association with the railway had disappeared almost as if it had never been. The close association between the village, the coal trade and the railway which had lasted for some 340 years was over.

Throughout the 1960s and 1970s the railway system in North-West Durham, as elsewhere in Britain, shrank or disappeared altogether. Of the Coal Board lines, the Chopwell and Garesfield and the Stella Unit in the Blaydon area had closed in 1961, the Team Way in 1963, the Beamish Railway followed in 1966 and the Bowes Railway ceased operation in 1974 when Kibblesworth colliery closed (*see map page 92*). The Tanfield branch ceased operation with the closure of Watergate colliery in 1964. The locomotive sheds at Borough Gardens and Blaydon which had long provided much of the motive power for the coal trains were closed by British Railways in 1959 and 1965 respectively. Gateshead Shed remained operational but it was largely concerned with passenger and long-distance goods traffic. The Derwent Valley line to Blackhill, lost its passengers service on 1st February, 1954 and was closed completely on 11th November, 1963; the track had been lifted by 1965. Consett Iron Works closed in 1980 and the town's last remaining rail link, to Ouston Junction on the ECML, closed in 1983. The Swalwell branch survived until the late 1980s being used as a disposal site for opencast coal.

At Dunston the line from Norwood to Dunston East Junction was closed on 1st June, 1970 and the large Norwood Junction signal box followed on 16th December, 1973; the line from Norwood to the staiths closed on 26th May, 1980 and the tracks in the coal yard and most of those on the staiths were lifted. The coal yard area together with the now vacant sites of the gas works and the Redheugh Iron and Steel Co. were cleared and detoxified to provide the location for the National Garden Festival of 1990, as remarkable a transformation as one could imagine. An interesting feature of the Festival was the tram line laid between Norwood Junction and the restored staiths. The Redheugh branch to the east of the Atlas Curve was reduced to a single track, eventually to disappear together with the many private sidings it once served. Dunston goods station survived until 1965, but of the long-closed passenger station only the derelict, weed-grown platform remained. It seemed inevitable that the remaining rail lines through Dunston would also be abandoned. However it was not to be.

The network of routes around the village which had been developed to serve the coal traffic and local industry, now ensured the continuation of the long association of the railway and Dunston. Probably the single most important factor was the existence of the Dunston to Gateshead link which, with the connecting Derwenthaugh branch, duplicated the Scotswood section of the Carlisle line along the north side of the Tyne. The reduction in rail traffic

The final product. The MV *Lindo* moves out into the river from the Dunston staiths with coal for British Columbia, a 33 day journey via the Panama Canal.   *K. Groundwater*

Norwood yard on 8th April, 1977. Loaded mineral wagons await the next ship, whilst the empty wagons have been run off the staiths in the distance.   *John Mallon*

through the abandonment of much of its general freight business, led British Rail to simplify its system by rerouting the Carlisle traffic over the King Edward Bridge and through Dunston to join the original main line at Blaydon from 4th October, 1982. Scotswood rail bridge was closed and the rails and bridge deck removed but the girders were left in place to carry some water mains. The line north of the Tyne through Scotswood was reduced to a single track serving Stella North Power Station and the Forth Engineer's sidings.

In 1984 approval was given to reopen Dunston passenger station as an unmanned halt which event followed on the 1st October that year. A second new station on the line was opened in 1987 to serve the Metro Centre, the large shopping complex which had been built partly on the site of the ash ponds of Dunston 'B' Power Station, a new enterprise arising literally from the ashes of the old! In 1996 the Metro Centre station had no less than 47 weekday trains westbound and 49 eastbound, many serving Sunderland and Carlisle as well as Newcastle and with some connecting services to places as far away as Middlesborough, Glasgow and Stranraer. In marked contrast the Dunston service had deteriorated from the 14 trains in each direction daily in 1990 to only a single daily train each way. The one daily train 'service' seems to be a ploy to avoid the necessity and trouble of officially closing the station for the third time in its history.

A new industrial enterprise appeared in the early 1990s when an access line was built on the route of the original Atlas Curve to service Shepherd's Scrap Yard on the Tyne bank.

With the electrification of the ECML (originally planned by the NER just after World War I) and the consequent reorganisation and simplification of the railway system around Newcastle Central, the Bensham Curve was closed and the

Dunston Extension line between Low Fell and Norwood Junctions was reduced to single track, signalled for two-way working. Part of this stretch of line has been electrified to give access by ECML postal traffic to sidings serving the new Royal Mail Hub at Low Fell, opened by the Post Office on 6th March, 1995.

The attractions of the Tyne valley to the west of Newcastle both as a place to live and for recreation and the importance of the Newcastle-Carlisle line as the only cross-country rail route between York and Liverpool to the south and Edinburgh and Glasgow to the north, should ensure its survival for the foreseeable future. New and upgraded stations and park-and-ride facilities have been proposed for the line to relieve congestion on the A69 road. A late mining development has been the opening of an open-cast mine at Plenmeller near Haltwhistle. The coal is railed to the old Bates staith at Blyth for export, the coal trains passing through Dunston to cross the Tyne by the King Edward Bridge; the long association of the village with the railway and coal traffic it seems has not quite ended.

The growth of the rail network around Dunston in the late 19th century to reach its maximum extent early in the 20th century well illustrates the way in which the needs of the coal trade could influence and direct the development of the railway. The Dunston Extension and its connection to the Redheugh branch were built solely in response to the demands of the coal trade and the subsequent construction of the Derwenthaugh-Norwood-Gateshead route can be seen to be a logical development of the system. Whether the latter route would have ever been built if the original staiths scheme had not happened is debatable, but there is no doubt that the existence of a direct line between Derwenthaugh and the King Edward Bridge had a very significant effect in later years on the shape of the present-day rail network west of Newcastle and Gateshead. Despite the eventual demise of the mining and shipment of coal in the region, it has ensured the continuation of the long association of Dunston and the railway.

View from Redheugh Gas Works Jn on 27th March, 1977. The line to Redheugh goods station ran along the river wall, whilst Redheugh incline to Gateshead ran beyond the buffer stops, through the right-hand span of Redheugh bridge and below the arched approach span of King Edward bridge. *John Mallon*

Chapter Eighteen

Preservation

At their greatest extent in the first half of the 20th century, the railways around Dunston extended to over eight miles of double running track, all devoted almost entirely to mineral and goods traffic. This was matched by a considerable mileage of single track and sidings, both company owned and in private hands. The coal yard sidings alone had over three miles of track.

By 1990 this network had shrunk to less than 3½ miles of double track plus the mile of single track and the Post Office sidings between Norwood and Low Fell Junctions. Goods and mineral trains had almost disappeared, replaced by passenger traffic on what was now an important cross-country route.

What remains of the old system?

The most impressive relic to be preserved is the Dunston staiths, together with one of the loading chutes and some short lengths of rail track. The 'new side' which had earlier been cut down to jetty height has now been completely removed apart from short lengths at either end. Now the property of the Tyne and Wear Buildings Preservation Trust and handsomely endowed by Sir Robert McAlpine & Co., the staiths are still an impressive sight and are probably the largest timber structure in Europe. However, to anyone who knew them in their heyday, they have a somewhat forlorn look, lacking wagons and locomotives, ships, dirt and coal dust and the noise of shunted wagons, engine whistles and ship sirens. The great embankment which constituted the coal yard can still be seen.

Of the once continuous belt of industry which covered the Tyne bank from the gas works to the mouth of the Derwent, virtually nothing remains. Old Ordnance Survey maps of the area, such as the series of reprints produced by Alan Godfrey, show just how much has disappeared.

Much of the abandoned rail network in the area can be traced both on the ground and by use of the Ordnance Survey 'Pathfinder' series of maps. The roadbed of the Derwent valley line is now the 'Derwent Walk' and can be followed from the site of the old Swalwell station as far as Blackhill. Much of the route of the NER line from Leadgate eastwards through Stanley to its one-time junction with the ECML and beyond towards Washington can be traced, while sections of the older, heavily graded line of the Stanhope and Tyne Railway between Stanley and Pelton can still be identified. The route of the Pontop and Jarrow/Bowes Railway may be followed as a cycleway from its old crossing point on the Tanfield branch at Marley Hill across the Team valley to Blackham's Hill where the stationary engine-worked incline has been preserved and may be seen operating on working days. The early waggonways (other than the Tanfield described below) are more difficult to locate but can in part be traced with help of the excellent details given in the book *A Fighting Trade* (*see Bibliography*).

103

Marley Hill on a Tanfield Railway 'Gala' day in 1986; a fine collection of restored industrial engines are to be seen. From the left the working locomotives are *Irwell*, *Cecil A. Cochrane*, *Armstrong*, *Whitworth* diesel 'No. 2', *Hawthorn*, *Leslie* 'No. 2' and *Robert Stephenson*, *Hawthorn* 'No. 38'. *A.R. Thompson*

The Tanfield Railway. A pair of typical industrial locomotives. *Sir Cecil A. Cochrane* (ex-Gateshead Gas Works) and *Irwell* at Marley Hill station on a train of 19th century passenger coaches. *A.R. Thompson*

Preserved Locomotives

Of the NER locomotive types which worked around Dunston, Wilson Worsdell's class 'P3') (LNER 'J27') and Raven's class 'T2' (LNER 'Q6') were the last pre-Grouping engines to remain in normal service in Britain. Ideally suited for their work some of each class survived into 1967 still engaged in the heavy mineral haulage they were designed for, having outlived many newer, more glamorous and better known engines.

Appropriately, one of each type has been preserved. Built at Darlington in 1923, 'P3' NER No. 2392 spent much of its working life at York before before ending its days at Sunderland in 1967. Also from Darlington and built in 1918, 'T2' NER No. 2238 was stationed at Blaydon in 1923 before moving to Selby and Consett. It also was finally withdrawn from Sunderland in 1967. Both engines were acquired by the North Yorkshire Moors Railway where they have been modified by fitting the vacuum brake and screw couplings to enable them to haul passenger stock, a duty they never performed during their earlier working life.

One of the class 'E1' (LNER 'J72') 0-6-0 tank engines of the type which worked in the Dunston coal yard and on the staiths has also survived, again hauling passengers and sporting the name *Joem* although very few NER locomotives were ever named. This particular engine was one of the series built by British Railways in 1949/51. The Beamish Open Air Museum owns a T.W. Worsdell 0-6-0 tender engine NER No. 876 class 'C' (LNER 'J21') built at Gateshead in 1889. This engine was stationed at Blaydon Shed in the 1950s. The class 'C' was one of the NER's most numerous and successful engines being used for both passenger and goods traffic. They were often seen on special trains and would almost certainly have appeared occasionally at Dunston on excursions. Of the privately-owned locomotives which worked in the area, five have been preserved. Two, both 0-4-0 saddle tanks, were from the Dunston power stations, another saddle tank (now on the Tanfield Railway) and a diesel-mechanical type were from the Redheugh gas works and the last was an ex-NER 0-4-0 which had worked for the National Coal Board at Watergate colliery.

The Tanfield Railway

Part of the old Tanfield branch has fortunately been preserved as the Tanfield Railway, established in 1971. The Railway, the oldest operating line in the world, is based on what is probably the oldest functioning locomotive shed, built in 1854 at Marley Hill by the Pontop & Jarrow Railway. The worked part of the line runs from Sunniside southwards past Marley Hill and the Causey Arch to East Tanfield. The Trust owns a number of locomotives, chiefly four- or six-wheeled saddle tanks, most of which were built or worked in the North East. One, *Sir Cecil A. Cochrane* built by Robert Stephenson & Hawthorn's in 1948 originally served at the Redheugh Gas Works. The oldest is a 0-4-0 saddle tank, built in 1873 by Black, Hawthorn in Gateshead. The passenger stock includes a North Eastern Railway inspection saloon of 1874 and a selection of restored four-wheeled carriages. The Marley Hill Shed which is well equipped for the restoration and maintenance of steam locomotives also does work for other preserved railways and for the nearby Beamish Open Air Museum. Although the track of the Bowes Railway to the east of Marley Hill has been lifted, the level crossing with the Tanfield line has been rebuilt, together with a replica of the tiny NER signal box which controlled it. The sidings at Marley Hill display two of the later type of iron-wheeled chaldron waggons (ex-Londonderry Railway) as well as a remarkable collection of rescued locomotives and rolling stock awaiting restoration, either to full working order or cosmetically.

In addition to the working stretch of the railway, cycleways and footpaths have been established along the route of the branch from Sunniside to near the foot of the Lobley Hill incline, although the lower end of the incline has been obliterated by the motorway. The site of the unique Teams Crossing where the Tanfield and Teams waggonways crossed can be identified by the roundabout at the junction of Ellison Road and the modern road which has replaced Clockmill Lane. At Causey the Arch has been restored from its earlier sorry state and a replica of a wooden-wheeled chaldron waggon standing on wooden track may be seen. The Arch as built had no parapets and modern metal railings have necessarily been added for the safety of visitors walking over it. The valley of the Causey Burn is now heavily wooded, largely obscuring the view of the Arch, and also making it difficult to appreciate the magnitude of the great embankment. The scale of the Arch itself is best realised when viewed from below from the footpath along the western side of the valley.

The Tanfield Railway. The diminutive *Irwell* heads north towards Sunniside with a train of vintage carriages. The curve to the right was the connecting loop between the Tanfield branch and the Bowes Railway and the replica of the tiny NER signal box which controlled the crossing of the two lines can be seen in the distance.   *A.R. Thompson*

The Beamish North of England Open Air Museum

This magnificent museum gives the visitor some idea of what life was like in the mining areas of the North East in the early years of the 20th century. The only things missing are soot and dirt!

The coal mining exhibit includes a re-opened part of the Mahogany Drift mine dating from the 1850s, where visitors can experience the atmosphere of an underground coal mine and see various mining methods demonstrated. Nearby a typical group of pithead buildings including an engine house, heapstead and screens has been re-erected, while Francis Street is a row of pit cottages brought from Hetton-le-Hole where they were lived in until the 1970s. The colliery site also displays a number of industrial locomotives and chaldron waggons from various locations in Durham. Of particular interest are the working replica of *Locomotion* the engine which opened the Stockton and Darlington Railway in 1825, and George Stephenson's Hetton locomotive built in 1822 and which continued in work until the early years of the 20th century.

The railway station site (the station itself came from Rowley) contains examples of NER buildings and equipment including signals, signal box and coal cells. The cast-iron footbridge which connects the station platform with the goods yard came from Dunston staiths. The preserved NER class 'C' locomotive may be seen here showing what a steam engine could look like, clean and in the full glory of late Victorian livery. NER rolling stock exhibits include one of the distinctive high-sided 20 ton coal hoppers, a brake van and a clerestory-roofed, brake composite (i.e. 1st, 3rd and guard's compartments) non-corridor passenger coach built at York in 1903 and similar to the type of carriage modified for auto-train working.

The preserved NER class 'C' 0-6-0 locomotive at Beamish. Built at Gateshead Works in 1989 this engine was withdrawn from service from South Blyth in 1962 having been stationed at Blaydon in the late 1950s. *Author*

Preserved wagons at Beamish. The one at the left is one of the very distinctive NER 20 ton wooden hoppers. In actual service it would have been a good deal dirtier than it now appears! A pair of NER vans flank a 'foreigner' from the Great Western Railway while to the right of the picture is an early type of NER brake van with a 'birdcage' lookout on the roof for the guard. The signal is an early type NER wooden, slotted-post shunting signal.

Author

A frequent service of trams, including a Gateshead Tramways single deck car similar to the type which ran the Dunston service from the 1920s until 1951, connects the main museum sites.

For some 500 years Durham County was largely dependent, directly or indirectly, upon the mining and export of coal. At Beamish the beautifully maintained Pockerley Manor and the Home Farm are reminders that even in the heyday of the coal industry, the county was by no means entirely given over to pits, slag heaps and coal dust.

Appendix One

Weights and Measures Used in the North Eastern Coal Trade

Throughout this book weights and measures have been given in Imperial units as being appropriate to the period. Tons have not been converted to tonnes as the difference is hardly significant when the original weights (except in modern times) were themselves usually only approximations or estimates. While given as weights, many of the measures were in fact measures of volume, and in addition were commonly treated in a cavalier fashion, as for example, heaping the coal in a waggon or even adding extra boards to the sides, so as to increase its capacity above the size agreed upon when negotiating wayleave rents. In particular, the ten, the unit used in determining wayleave charges and colliery output, varied greatly between collieries.

The basic unit in the coal trade was the boll or bowle, a measure of volume, officially 6 bushells, each of 8 gallons, the actual weight depending upon the product being measured; a boll of coal weighed about 2.2 cwt, roughly 112kg.

Traditional Measure	Metric Equivalent (approximate)
A pack horse could carry about 2 cwt	100 kg
A cart or cowp carried 3¾ bolls = 8¼ cwt	420 kg
A wain carried 1 fother = 7½ bolls = 17½ cwt	890 kg
A keel carried 8 waggon loads, about 21 tons	20,000 kg
A Newcastle chaldron in 1616 was 43 cwt	2,190 kg
A Newcastle chaldron in 1678 was 52½ cwt	2,670 kg
A Newcastle chaldron in 1695 was 53 cwt	2,698 kg
A London chaldron was 25½ cwt	1,294 kg

The ten was set by agreement between the landowner and the coalowner or lessee at so many waggons of a given capacity and could range from 20 to 33 waggons carrying from about 300 to over 500 bolls! For example:

A Gibside ten was 42 fothers of 7½ bolls or about 37 tons.
A Bucksnook ten was 21 waggons of 19 bolls or about 44 tons.

Appendix Two

Tonnage of Coal and Coke Shipped at Dunston Staiths 1893 to 1926

Year	Tonnage	Notes
1893-4	684,070	Average per annum.
1895-9	1,308,640	Average per annum.
1900	1,351,480	
1901	1,428,927	
1902	1,502,820	
1903	2,054,928	
1904	2,463,810	
1905	2,830,588	
1906	3,044,876	
1907	3,268,794	
1908	3,408,750	
1909	3,593,568	
1910	3,412,774	Miners strike 3rd January to 15th April.
1911	3,523,268	
1912	2,920,596	Miners strike 26th February to 15th April.
1913	3,042,498	
1914	2,776,380	World War I.
1915	2,607,033	World War I.
1916	2,169,547	World War I.
1917	1,676,067	World War I.
1918	1,401,690	World War I.
1919	1,729,612	
1920	1,520,420	
1921	1,808,682	Coal strike 1921.
1922	3,279,662	
1923	4,061,413	
1924		Figures not available.
1925		Figures not available.
1926	1,694,408	General strike.

Bibliography

Allen C.J., *The North Eastern Railway*, Ian Allan, London, 1964

Bennett G., Clavering E. & Rounding A., *A Fighting Trade - Rail Transport in Tyne Coal 1600-1800*, Portcullis Press, Gateshead, 1990
A fascinating and carefully researched account of the history of the coal trade and the early waggonways in North-West Durham and the people who built them. Includes details and maps of the routes and present day remains.

Cook R.A. & Hoole K., *North Eastern Railway Historical Maps*, Railway & Canal Historical Society, 1975

Elliott John A., *Private Owner Wagons of the North-East Vol. 1 The Chaldrons*, Chilton Iron Works, Houghton-le-Spring, 1994

Essery, R.J., Rowland D.P. & Steel W.O., *British Goods Wagons - From 1887 to the Present Day*, David & Charles, Newton Abbot 1970

Faith, Nicholas, *The World the Railways Made*, Pimlico, 1994

Groundwater P. & K., 'Coal by Rail, the Staiths at Dunston-on-Tyne' in *Railway World*, 1984

Hair, T.H., *Sketches of the Coal Mines in Durham and Northumberland*, Frank Graham (reprint), Newcastle-upon-Tyne, 1969.
A facsimile reprint of a 1844 publication.

Hearse, G.S., *The Tramways of Gateshead*, G.S. Hearse, Corbridge, 1965

Hoole, K., *North Eastern Locomotive Sheds*, David & Charles, Newton Abbot, 1972

Hoole, K., *Railway Stations of the North East*, David & Charles, Newton Abbot, 1985

Hoole, K., *An Illustrated History of NER Locomotives*, Haynes Publishing Group, Sparkford, near Yeovil, 1988

Hoole, K., *Rail Centres – Newcastle*, Ian Allan, 1986

Lee, C. E., 'The World's Oldest Railway' in *Transactions of the Newcomen Society*, Vol. 25, 1945-47, Courier Press, Leamington Spa, 1950

Lewis, M.J.T., *Early Wooden Railways*, Routledge & Kegan Paul, London 1970
A detailed and scholarly history of the origins and development of the early waggonways in Europe and Britain.

Mountford, C. & Charlton, L.G., *Industrial Locomotives of Durham*, Handbook 'L', Industrial Railway Society, Market Harborough, 1977
An excellent source of information about both the locomotives and the industrial sites they served.

Mountford, C., *The Bowes Railway*, Industrial Railway Society, Tyne & Wear Industrial Monuments Trust, 1976

Shaw, S., *A Pictorial Essay Produced to Commemorate the National Garden Festival 1990*, Gateshead MBC Education Department, Gateshead, 1990
Excellent illustrations but some inaccuracies in the text.

Smith, R., *History of the Coal Factors in the London Market*, Longmans 1961

Tatlow, P., *A Pictorial Record of LNER Wagons*, Oxford Publishing Co. Ltd, 1976

Tomlinson, W.W., *The North Eastern Railway, Its Rise and Development*, David & Charles, Newton Abbot (reprint), 1967
The classical history of the North Eastern Railway. Unfortunately poor health prevented the author from completing his work and the 20th century developments are sketched in and do not extend beyond 1914.

Warn, C.R., *Rails Between Tyne & Wear*, Frank Graham, Newcastle-upon-Tyne, (no date).

Whittle, G., *The Newcastle and Carlisle Railway*, David & Charles, Newton Abbot, 1979

Whittle, G., *The Railways of Consett and North-West Durham*, David & Charles, Newton Abbot, 1971

The quarterly Journal of the North Eastern Railway Association, the *North Eastern Express*, is a mine of information on the railways of the North East, past and present. The reprints of old large-scale Ordnance Survey Maps produced by Alan Godfrey have been an invaluable, and detailed source of information about the changes which have occurred in the region over the last hundred years.

Index